Sent Forth to Minister

True Angel Stories

Vera Overholt

Thank You

- To each of you who have shared your personal experiences and encounters with angels.

- To my daughters, Abigail Berryman and Sarah Alimowski, for designing, editing and proofreading this publication, and to all who helped with typing and proofreading.

- To my family, for your support, counsel and stories.

Sent Forth to Minister © 2016 The Christian Hymnary Publishers
Third Edition – 2017
ISBN 978-0-9728009-6-9

For additional information, contact the publisher:
P.O. Box 51955 Sarasota, Florida 34232

Introduction

H ave you ever seen an angel, or felt an unmistakable, unseen presence? Or have you been helped by an angel in disguise, leaving you to wonder where "the person" had come from or where he had gone? As followers of God, we all experience the presence, protection and deliverance of angels – even when we are not aware of them! (Psalm 34:7; Psalm 91:11).

References to angels are mentioned 283 times in the Bible (KJV). We notice that angels do the work of God. God sends them on assignments to minister, to guide, to protect, to help, to encourage and to deliver messages. Angels are at work today as in days of Bible times. We must remember, however, that one thing the angels cannot do is save us from sin, just as no person can. Only God is able to do that through the atonement of His Son, Jesus Christ, who gave His life and His precious blood for everyone: *"The blood of Jesus Christ His Son cleanseth us from all sin"*(1 John 1:7). We must also remember that the Word of God is always the final authority in our lives above any angelic encounter; if from the Lord, these experiences will always be in harmony with His written Word (Gal. 1:8, 9; 2 Cor. 11:14).

Sometimes, in severe trials, testing, sickness and accidents, we may wonder where God and His angels were. But if we could have one glimpse into the unseen world, we would not question – for God and His angels were always there. He loves us, and His purposes in our lives are always loving, even when we do not understand His ways.

I have limited the stories in this book mostly to first-hand accounts from family, friends and relatives, rather than taking them from others' books. A number of stories were previously printed in my set of four *Scrapbook of Ideas for Christian Workers*.

I hope you will be inspired by these true stories, as I have, and become more sensitive to the supernatural ways of God: His still, small voice, His comforting, guiding Spirit and His ministering angels. May we put our trust wholly in the Lord, who directs His angels to help us in every area of need. ✺

Vera Overholt, Compiler, 2016
Sarasota, Florida

Table of Contents

"*A* re they not all
ministering spirits,
Sent Forth to Minister
for them who shall be
heirs of salvation?"

Hebrews 1:14

*A*LWAYS READY TO TAKE ACTION,
      TO OBEY THE LORD'S COMMAND,

*N*EVER LATE TO HEED HIS BIDDING,
      SERVING SAINTS IN EVERY LAND.

*G*OING WILLINGLY, GOD'S SERVANTS,
      QUICK TO DO THE MASTER'S WILL,

*E*VER FAITHFUL, WHEN HE SENDS THEM
      ON A MISSION TO FULFILL.

*L*OVINGLY THEY GUARD GOD'S CHILDREN,
      COMFORT AND PROTECT AND LEAD,

*S*UPERNATURAL, THESE STRONG WARRIORS
      WILL HELP ANYONE IN NEED.

- Abigail Berryman

1

A Child Sees Angels

"I, Jesus, have sent mine angel..." Revelation 22:16. "... Thou hast hid these things from the wise and prudent, and hast revealed them unto babes...." Luke 10:21

Nearly forty years have passed, and yet I remember the details as if it was yesterday. I was around five years old, and it was springtime in the quiet countryside of Waynesboro, Georgia, where we lived.

My mother was sitting at her sewing machine in the dining room of our brick house, which was just down the road from the farm where my dad was working. I was playing with my dolls in the same room where my mother was sewing. All of a sudden, a movement outside caught my attention.

I ran over to the double windows that looked out to our back yard. What I saw astounded me, for I had never seen anything like it before.

Walking around our house, there was a group of approximately fifteen figures, all dressed in long, white robes. Their faces were hazy so that I could not tell their gender. I do remember that some were larger in size than others. Since I was inside, I couldn't hear them, but they appeared to be singing or talking to each other, though they looked straight ahead as they walked.

"Mama!" I exclaimed, "Who are those people walking around our house?" She looked outside and replied, "There is no one outside the house."

I was intrigued by what I had seen but not afraid, and went back to playing with my dolls. Before long, I saw the same group walking around our house!

"There they are again, Mama," I called. "Who is walking around our house?" Once more, she patiently told me that there was no one walking outside.

After a third time of my seeing the same group of figures walking around the house and asking her who they were, my dear Mama said, "Carolyn, I think you are seeing *angels*." And then they were gone.

I find it ironic that as soon as my mother mentioned that they were angels, they disappeared. I was too young to know if any danger was looming on the horizon in our area, and have often wondered about the reason for their appearance. But this vivid occurrence stays with me, and even today, I can still see that band of angels circling our home. ❧

Carolyn Kurtz, 2015
Westminster, SC

A Child's Vision of Angels

As I was sorting through old files recently, I came across a note I had jotted down years ago. Around 1988, my four-year-old son was listening to a visiting minister preaching in Hartville, Ohio, when a scene formed on the wall behind the pulpit. My son saw Jesus in the clouds, surrounded by angels! But he could not see Jesus' face. It was an unforgettable experience for an impressionable little boy, who felt that God was telling us that He is coming soon. And it was a reminder for me, as a mother, to never underestimate the ways God chooses to speak to children. ❧

- Dover, Ohio

2

A Surprise Through the Window

"Take heed that ye despise not one of these little ones; for I say unto you, that in heaven their angels do always behold the face of my Father which is in heaven." Matthew 18:10

As told to me by Walentyna, my mother-in-law:

It was springtime in 1963, in our small, farming village of Narew, Poland. Only eighteen years had passed since the Second World War had ended, and our family and neighbors were still trying to recover from the ravaging horrors of the war. With Narew located less than an hour's drive west of the Russian border, our village had been caught in the crossfire of the opposing Russian and German armies, leaving many dead and destitute.

My husband, Jurek, and I worked hard on our farm to support our two little sons and my elderly parents, who lived with us at the time. It was planting season, and there was much to be done.

Around noon, one lovely day, I fed our baby, Marek, before putting him to sleep in his crib. Leaving *Babcia* (bahp-CHAH – *Grandmother*) to watch him, I went outside with my husband to work in the fields. I wasn't concerned leaving Marek in his grandmother's care, as she often helped take care of him. He was a quiet and sweet baby, making no trouble for her – he typically slept so quietly and so long that she would check on him to see if he was still alive!

After I had gone out, Babcia was rocking the crib and Marek was almost asleep. Suddenly, a shining light appeared at the window, and she saw an angel coming! He looked like she expected an angel would look – he was wearing white, his face was glowing and he was surrounded by light.

The angel came and stood over the crib, looking down at the baby. A feeling of peacefulness filled the room, and Babcia wondered if he was going to take Marek away. She didn't know what to think about it and was pondering what she should say to him. But before she had a chance to ask him anything, he suddenly left.

How surprised and blessed we all felt when Babcia told us what had happened. Who was this heavenly visitor, and what was the purpose of his visit? Was this Marek's guardian angel who was assigned by God to watch over him? ∾

Sarah Alimowski, 2014
North Port, FL

∾ Compiler's Note: In 2005, Marek, the baby in this story, married our daughter, Sarah. They now own the farm in Narew, Poland, where this story took place, and occasionally live there with their two sons, Samuel and Rafael, in the summer months.

All night, all day, angels watching over me, my Lord,
All night, all day, angels watching over me.
Sun is setting in the west; angels watching over me, my Lord,
Sleep my child, take your rest; angels watching over me.

– Author Unknown (believed to have originated in the southern
United States during the days of slavery)

3

Angel on Midway Street

"For it is written, 'He shall give His angels charge over thee, to keep thee…'"
Luke 4:10

Uncle Joe and my father, John – twin brothers – lived with their aged mother in the old, pre-Civil War farmhouse on Midway Street, in Hartville, Ohio. The stories and examples of the Early Church, the Anabaptist movements, the Moravians and the Wesley brothers had so inspired and infected them that they lived, breathed, ate and slept with the desire to impact and win others for Jesus. Their modus operandi was summed up in one word – souls. The lifelong pursuit of formal and self-education to better train teachers for Christian schools, equip missionaries with languages to effectively communicate the gospel and with necessary skills to disciple new believers, had made them teachers of the teachers.

In the rooms upstairs in the old farmhouse, and in the summer house behind, stood rows of wooden melon crates stacked high to the ceiling. They were packed with books, magazines, trinkets from some foreign country, and treasured keepsakes. But mostly books.

Grandmother Hannah moved on to glory and her reward in 1965, the same year that my father, age 46, got married to my mother, Vera Sommers, age 33, a loyal friend who was often involved in local and foreign singing ministry. Uncle Joe now had to move into the summer house to make way for his brother's new wife and burgeoning family – but the books remained. Five children, ages five and under, with the youngest born on my fifth birthday, severely stretched Father's bachelor reading and sleeping habits. So he often opted for the upstairs, spare bedroom, adjoining my brother Matthias' and mine.

Some of the melon crates contained past issues of LIFE and TIME magazines, whose pictorial coverage of the Vietnam War fascinated but also frightened me. It was 1972, and the smoldering embers of the bloody riots at nearby Kent State University (Mother's *alma mater*) and the bitter remains of a conflict that would not be decided, weighed heavily on the nation and found voice in daily living. War stories were quite normal in our house, since my father had worked for Mennonite Central Committee (MCC) in Poland, Germany and France, feeding and clothing refugees after World War II.

But, as a little six-year-old boy who didn't understand what was going on, I struggled with fear of the unknown and wanted to sleep with my father – to feel and connect with his strength. Mother set up a little hideaway bed near his bed, and I slept there during that period of my life when I was afraid.

One night, I was soundly sleeping on my cot, when all at once I awoke, and immediately found myself able to see through the wall to the outside. It was a pleasant, summer night and the gentle breeze caressed my skin. The fireflies flickered brightly and the lights of our neighbors, the Wengerds and the Haverstocks, cheerily lit the darkness. I smelled the fragrance of the peony bushes that lined our sidewalk and the blooming lilac bush on the corner of the lawn. I heard crickets merrily singing, leading the cadence of the nighttime chorus.

Suddenly, a gorgeous, white being descended, alighting on the road, not fifty feet from our front porch. Instantly I knew – *an angel!* (Mother had often read stories to us of angels, and both of my parents lived their lives with an awareness of the supernatural.

When they prayed, you could feel there was *Someone* out there – *there really was a God!*)

The angel didn't say anything to me or look in my direction, but I immediately sensed tranquility and peace and wonderment. As I stared in awe, I saw the brightly illuminated angel move slowly down the road toward Market Avenue, past the Yoder's place, to the stop sign near the Anderson's house, a quarter mile away. There it gently lifted up, gradually rising until it disappeared from sight.

My heart pounded with excitement and I leaped out of bed, and shook my sleeping father awake. "Father!" I loudly exclaimed, "I just saw an angel!" Now, looking back, I realize how easily my father could have squashed my heart. Instead, he rejoiced with me and exclaimed, "Son, that's *wonderful*! The Bible says, 'The angel of the Lord encamps around those who fear him and delivers them.' That's wonderful you saw an angel. I'm so happy for you!"

I lay back down, but I was so excited that I couldn't go back to sleep for a long time. As I tell this story now, 44 years later, I can visualize that unforgettable experience like it was yesterday. I can see the fireflies, feel and smell the warm, night air, and see the porch lights of the Wengerd's house across the street. And I can still see the angel who calmed the fears of a frightened little boy. ❧

Nathan Overholt, 2016
Sarasota, FL

> *...Angels descending bring from above,*
> *Echoes of mercy, whispers of love.*
> *This is my story, this is my song,*
> *Praising my Savior all the day long.*
>
> (Blessed Assurance - Fanny Crosby)

4

Peace in the Night

"Be strong and of a good courage, fear not, nor be afraid... for the Lord thy God, He it is that doth go with thee; He will not fail thee, nor forsake thee." Deut. 31:6. "And there appeared an angel unto him from heaven, strengthening him." Luke 22:43

It was the summer of 2000, and my husband, Laban, and I were preparing to move from Sarasota, Florida, to live near Laban's aging parents in northwestern Pennsylvania. They lived in the heavily wooded, scenic countryside of Cochranton, near the Alleghany Mountains.

It was a beautiful area, but I was struggling with the move. Florida had been home for fifteen years, and I would be moving away from my family, friends and church. I cried in private, trying to hide the emotional upheaval from my children and come to terms with this major life change.

In preparation for the move, we decided that Laban would drive to Cochranton with a couple of the children, and I would stay behind with the rest of the family. Twelve-year-old Aaron and my youngest, Abby, were excited about going along, nearly 1200 miles north to visit their grandparents. Breathing a prayer, I waved them off. *"Lord, please protect them and work things out for us."* Little did I imagine how He would reveal His care for us through an unforgettable event in our daughter's life.

Here is Abby's story:

"One evening, Aaron was acting as most brothers do, telling me scary stories just because he enjoyed seeing my reaction. Outside, the shadows from the woods around Grandpa's little stone cottage looked like lurking giants, and I felt anything but calm. Later that night, as everyone was in bed, I lay awake upstairs, unable to sleep. Aaron was fast asleep in his bed on the other side of the room, oblivious to the apprehension I was feeling as a result of his dramatic story-telling. I became overcome with fear and wished Mom was nearby, but she was far away in Florida. I felt anxiety unlike anything I had ever known before, and fear so real and tangible that I could feel the presence of evil. I was terrified!

As I lay there in bed, I began praying as strongly and sincerely as a little eight-year-old could. Suddenly, something caught my attention and I whipped around and saw the most beautiful sight that will forever be engraved in my memory. About six feet away from my bed stood the figure of a very tall person, glowing so brightly that I couldn't make out any other detail. The instant my eyes met the angel, all fear vanished, and I was consumed by the warmest and safest feelings that I had ever experienced. I do not know how long I lay there staring, mesmerized by this holy being, but I fell asleep with the angel standing there, enveloped by its loving presence.

When I awoke in the morning, I ran downstairs to tell Dad of my protector that appeared to me the night before. He believed me and thought it was amazing! When Grandpa and Grandma heard it, they didn't say much or seem surprised. The following day was Sunday, and I asked Dad to share my story at their congregation, which he did. I was so excited about what had happened and wanted everyone to know. Since Dad often told me angel stories before bedtime, I fully believed that I could see one anytime. But then it actually happened to me, and now I have my own angel story to tell!"

When Abby called me to tell me about her encounter with the angel, I was stunned. *This always happens to other people, not someone in our family! What is the meaning of this?* I pressed Abby for more specifics, asking many questions. As she relayed the details, I knew she was telling the truth, since she was not inclined to fabricate stories.

While pondering her angelic visitor, I thought about the story I had heard about the appearance of an angel to my husband's sister, Rhoda, years earlier. As a 3-year-old child, an angel came to her when she was very ill. When she told her mother she had seen an angel, her mother asked what the angel looked like. Little Rhoda pointed to the paper angel that she had made in Sunday school, which was sitting on the dresser, and said the angel looked just like that. *Is this why Laban's parents didn't react more or seem surprised when Abby told them her story? Were they thinking back to their own daughter's visit by an angel, and trying to comprehend the meaning?*

In the following days, I continued to reflect on our daughter's divine encounter. I was in awe of how close God is when we don't realize it. He sees our fears, and desires to show Himself to us. Just as His angel cared for Abby in my absence, He would be there for me, regardless what the future held, and give me the courage I needed to face the changes ahead. ❧

Bonnie Kurtz, 2016
Sarasota, FL

❧ Compiler's Note: In January, 2016, after living in Cochranton, PA, for 15 years, Bonnie experienced another difficult life change, following the sudden and unexpected death of her husband, Laban. She moved back to Florida and lives with her mother, Mrs. Andrew Overholt. As she walks through this valley of grief and change, she continues to lean on the One she has learned to trust - not understanding *why*, but finding strength to go on, one day at a time.

5
The Night Guardian

"And he dreamed, and behold a ladder set up on the earth, and the top of it reached to heaven: and behold the angels of God ascending and descending on it. And Jacob awaked out of his sleep, and he said, 'Surely the LORD is in this place...'" Gen. 28:12, 16

When I was a little girl, around six years old, I lived with my family in the rural outskirts of Sarasota, a growing city on the Gulf Coast of Florida. We had moved there when I was five, in 1970, when my dad was asked to help pastor Sunnyside Fellowship, a newly forming Amish Mennonite congregation. It had not been an easy decision for my parents to move their family from a peaceful, farming community in Plain City, Ohio, to the city; and so soon after returning from Belize, where they had been involved in mission work and church planting for over seven years, and where four of us children were born.

But God had clearly called my parents to move to Florida, and confirmed it through a poem my dad had read about giving up the fields for the crown, and the many people needing Jesus in the city. So here we were, once again living in a sunny, humid climate, in a small house that had been converted from a milking parlor. The 30-acre dairy farm had been purchased to build the Sunnyside Nursing home, a ministry to the elderly where young people could come for a term of voluntary service.

Living near the bustling activities of the nursing home, we had lots of people coming and going and often interacted with the voluntary service workers. We made new friends, and had fun playing with the neighbor children, whose parents were also involved in some way in the ministry of the nursing home. On Sundays, we met for worship in the nursing home chapel, with some of the staff and elderly residents also in attendance, and my dad pastored the budding congregation. And so the days in our new Florida home passed happily for me as a little girl.

But one night in particular is etched in my memory, which I will never forget. Darkness had fallen, and everything was quiet inside our little house. The nocturnal sounds of the subtropics filtering through the windows had lulled everyone into tranquil sleep. I was fast asleep in the upper bunk bed, and my sisters, Rhoda and Ruth, were peacefully dreaming below. Next to our bunk bed was a partition wall which Dad had built to divide our room into another small bedroom, where my older brother, Joseph, was also soundly sleeping.

Sometime during the night, something awoke me, and I drowsily opened my eyes. Suddenly, I was wide awake! Right in front of me, a large white form was hovering in the two-foot space above the partition wall that separated our bedrooms! I knew immediately it was an angel. It was glowing white all over and its wings were spread out. I wasn't scared as I looked at the angel but felt a sense of peacefulness and calm. I blinked my eyes, and then the angel was gone! No one else roused but continued in blissful slumber, unaware of the angelic guardian I had just seen. I went back to sleep and didn't wake anyone, but told them later what had happened.

Over the years, I have often pondered the reason the angel appeared to me. Was it to let me know that God is real, or to reassure a little girl that angels are watching over us, even in the nighttime? ❧

Rita Slabaugh, 2016
Nappanee, IN

❧ Compiler's Note: For many years, Rita's father, Brother Lester Gingerich, served as our bishop at Sunnyside Fellowship, and our family is grateful for his guidance and encouragement over the years and for giving us a church home. Recently a 45-year commemoration was held for Lester and Sarah, honoring their faithful years of ministry.

In 1967, my brother-in-law, Will Overholt, purchased the land to build Sunnyside Nursing Home, to provide a Christian home for the elderly and an Anabaptist service unit where our young men could complete their 1W service. It was an operating voluntary service unit for nine years, providing our young people a place to serve in VS work.

6

A Brave Soldier of God

"My God hath sent His angel, and hath shut the lions' mouths, that they have not hurt me: forasmuch as before Him innocency was found in me; and also before thee, O king, have I done no hurt." Daniel 6:22

The story of Daniel in the lions' den is a favorite Bible story of many children. Daniel was among the Hebrews in Jerusalem who were captured and taken to Babylon during the reign of the powerful king, Nebuchadnezzar.

Daniel faced many trials courageously, along with the other Israelites who had become Babylonian slaves. He was a talented young man and stood for truth, even though he was surrounded by pagan idolatry. He was an example that others could look up to.

Years later, Babylon became part of the kingdom of Persia, and Darius was the king. Darius set over his kingdom 120 princes and appointed three presidents, and chose Daniel to be the highest in authority.

This made the princes and the other two presidents very jealous. What could they do that would harm his reputation and remove him from his position of leadership? They watched him closely, but could find nothing of which to accuse him.

Finally, the leaders decided on a plan to find some fault relating to his religion and godly life. They went to the king and asked that he would make a law that for thirty days, no one should ask anything of any other god except from him, or else that person would be thrown into the lions' den. This pleased King Darius. He felt so honored and esteemed that he granted their petition.

But, in spite of the new law, Daniel continued to kneel and pray to God in heaven three times a day, looking toward Jerusalem as he prayed. His accusers reported this to the king.

King Darius was greatly distressed! He couldn't eat or sleep. He liked Daniel and did not want him to be harmed. He tried by every means to have the law annulled, but the leaders reminded him that he could not do that.

So Daniel was thrown into the den of lions. And here is the exciting part. God sent His angel and shut the lions' mouths! They did not hurt him or even roar. Did God send one of His special angels, like Gabriel or Michael, for this task?

The next morning, at the crack of dawn, King Darius went to the den and called Daniel. What a relief to the king that Daniel was still alive! Then the king made a rule that in every part of his kingdom, people would reverence the God of Daniel. ❧

Vera Overholt, 2016
Sarasota, FL

❧ Compiler's Note: Story adapted from Daniel 6:1-28

7

Angels in Guerrilla Strongholds

"For He shall give His angels charge over thee, to keep thee in all thy ways."
Psalm 91:11

"No tiene usted temor?" (*"Aren't you afraid?"*) Jaimie whispered hoarsely. Through the blackness of the night, I could scarcely see the youthful outline of his face as we trekked down the rutted trail on the guerrilla-infested mountainside. The hands on my watch had long passed the 6:00 curfew the remote villages had imposed during the peak of the 36-year guerrilla warfare terrorizing the country of Guatemala. Leftist rebels had incited Mayan indigenous poor to fight against the corrupt Guatemalan government. Much of the terrorism took place back in these mountains, in the communities surrounding Mennonite Air Mission's earliest churches. When I had landed at Guatemala City Airport the previous day, I noticed the empty souvenir shops. Few ventured out unnecessarily these days. Back in these hills – far from the lights, the police and the army of the larger cities – villagers lived on edge, never knowing when a band of terrorists would swoop in and capture or kill their men.

I switched off my dimming flashlight, trying to walk quietly enough to avoid alerting any lurking terrorists, and yet not too stealthily so as to startle the night patrol, guarding the slumbering village ahead. (They would shoot first and investigate later).

I hope Mark found the parts to fix the "Beast," I thought, thinking of the broken-down vehicle that had been custom built to travel these rugged roads. No one should have been out in these hills in the darkness – the hours when the abductions, violent tortures and murders took place, and bodies were dumped over the side of the mountain. But the journey was taking much longer than I had figured when we left the disabled vehicle beside the road.

"Aren't you afraid?" my travelling companion asked. I whispered back. "Through my mind keeps going the verse, *'the angel of the Lord encampeth around them that fear Him and delivereth them.'* No, I am not afraid. Many times the angels are all around us, protecting us, and we are not aware they are there. Once in a while the Heavenly Beings make their presence known, but often they work quietly, unseen. I think they are here tonight."

Somewhere ahead was a dirt landing strip where Harold, the mission pilot, had landed the plane on a night as dark as this. The boundaries of the airstrip were designated only by a motorcycle headlight at one end, and the lights of a pickup at the other. Somehow, while Christians in the village were desperately praying, Harold brought the plane down, missing the trees hidden in the darkness. There were angels around San Andrés that night, too.

On we trudged, sloshing through streams and crossing several low mountains, hoping we were still following the path to San Andrés. Somewhere ahead lay the village, where my friend, Pastor Ismael and his family slept in their adobe home. I scanned the darkness for signs of movement or the outline of the armed night patrol on duty. But all was still. I saved the last of the flashlight's batteries for the moment we would encounter the patrol keeping watch for the lurking terrorists.

The angel of the Lord... they were around, I knew it. I had sensed them before. I thought of one of my earlier trips to San

Bartolomè that lay across the mountains from here. For three hours, I had ridden on the back of the only vehicle daring to risk running the gauntlet of the guerrilla-occupied territory of the mountains of the Department of Quichè. In San Bartolomè, I had walked through the crowded streets, observing the heavy loads of vegetables balanced on the heads of the women arrayed in their native finery, and men with tall stacks of firewood on their backs, carried several hours over the mountains. Without a trace of fear, I had walked through the town, absorbing scents and sights, burdened that only a very few experienced forgiveness of sins. Later that day, as I enjoyed a meal with the pastor and his wife, they told me that several days before, they heard shouts. Looking out the window, they saw a group of men being herded through town. A few minutes later gunshots rang out. Village men discovered the bodies of the victims stuffed into black, body bags, lying at the bottom of the ravine. The pastor showed me the field of fresh graves – all victims of the guerrillas who had killed over 100 men in San Bartolomè alone. Suddenly I realized how conspicuous I must have been, a lone white man walking unarmed through the village where violence and murder was commonplace. Did I have an angel unawares?

As Jaimie and I continued walking through the rough terrain, I thought of the bus I had seen not long ago that lost its wheel, skidded to a stop, hung suspended, balanced for a moment and then landed right side up. The very next day, I jumped on a crowded bus headed west. After several hours, I changed buses at Los Encuentros, riding one of the "chicken buses" which raced each other around the hairpin curves, up and down the ravines – no guardrails? No. The crumpled skeleton of a hapless bus or two lay at the bottom of the cliffs as we careened around those tight hairpin curves. At Santa Cruz del Quiche, for the last leg of my journey, I had found only a heavily loaded pickup going to San Andrés. The muddy, rutted roads of the rainy season made the route impossible for the buses to traverse the mountainous road. After we had travelled for a spell, without warning, the right front wheel of the heavily loaded pickup gave way, and we skidded to a stop. Had the hand of an angel kept the wheel in place as we careened around those tight, hairpin curves? There were no guardrails in those days – just sheer drop-offs into endless ravines!

"No tengo temor" (*"I'm not afraid"*), I whispered as Jaimie and I trudged on toward San Andrès, somewhere in the darkness ahead. "No. Tengo en mi mente este versiculo *El ángel de Jehová acampa en derredor de los que le temen, Y los defiende*. (*Over and over this verse comes to mind: "The angel of the LORD encampeth round about them that fear him, and delivereth them." Psalm 34:7*).

Cresting a final hill, I could faintly make out the vague outline of the Catholic church steeple surrounded by tin-roofed, adobe huts in the village of San Andrès, wrapped in its blanket of total darkness. I switched on my dim flashlight. Spread out just ahead I could make out the forms of men of the night patrol, sprawled out, fast asleep. *What shall we do?* I silently wondered. *Should we try to sneak quietly around them? No. Though some of the guns are likely carved from wood, there is sure to be at least one loaded rifle.*

Shining my flashlight around, I loudly called out, "*Buenas noches!*" (*"Good Evening!"*) One, and only one man sat up, and sleepily mumbled "*Buenas noches,*" and flopped back down. In amazed unbelief, Jaimie and I walked right on through, wondering about the men we had encountered. No one was watching? No one was guarding this entrance to the sleeping town? But we, Jaimie and I, had guardian angels watching, guarding us, I was confident.

We found our way to the darkened mission house, and knocked at the door. Ismael asked, "*Quièn està afuera?*" (*"Who's there?"*)

Jaimie answered, since he had been there just a few months before. Ismael didn't recognize his voice, and asked again, *"Quièn està afuera?"*

This time, I answered. *"Hay dos àngeles afuera"* (*"There are two angels outside"*).

Amazingly, Ismael recognized my voice, though I had not been there for several years. He threw open the door and warmly welcomed us into his home. He switched on the light and called his family, who listened to our experiences, while his wife, Selma prepared food for us, with the skill with which she is widely known.

Sometime after I left Guatemala, I received word that the cattle truck, loaded with passengers traveling to San Bartolomè, had been targeted by the terrorists. As the truck travelled through a lonely spot, the terrorists, who were hiding behind the bank, detonated dynamite, propelling truck parts, shrapnel and body parts through the air. One of the few survivors was Josè, the native pastor at San Bartolomè, who had felt prompted to ask to sit in the cab of the truck instead of riding on the back. That change doubtlessly saved his life.

And then there was unfaithful Modesto, the first deacon from San Bartolomè. He denied the faith and encountered guerrillas first hand, and was killed in a dreadful way.

Later, in the same town, lived poor Bartolo. First, the guerrillas came to his home, trying to coerce him to join their gang. When Bartolo refused, the guerillas threatened to return in fifteen days. Exactly fifteen days later, Bartolo's family had gone to bed when angry shouts and stones pelting the tin roof announced the terrorists had returned.

While Bartolo's family cried out to God in their hut, Bartolo went out to face the terrorists. A gunshot blasted the night, and Bartolo collapsed to the ground. He felt no pain, but felt blood pouring out of the wound in his head, and down over his face. Looking up, Bartolo saw angels hovering above him. *"Have angels come to carry me to heaven?"* he wondered. Again, a terrorist raised his gun, and Bartolo braced for the fatal shot. Sensing someone kneeling at his side, he turned to see a man in the whitest robe who spoke softly, "Son, do not fear, because I am with you. You are blessed because you are doing My will."

The gunshot boomed, echoing through the village as Bartolo saw Jesus blowing away the pellets from the hand-loaded shell. Screaming in fright, the terrorists vanished, disappearing into the night. Minutes later, Bartolo knocked on the door of his house, calling for his wife to open. "Jesus carried me," he told her.

Yes, whether or not we saw them as we walked through the mountains that dark night, heavenly beings were hovering near. ❧

Urie Sharp, 2016
Bolivar, OH

*"Also I say unto you,
whosoever shall confess me before men,
him shall the Son of man also confess
before the angels of God:
But he that denieth me before men
shall be denied
before the angels of God."*
Luke 12:8, 9

8

Angels Over Waslala

"The chariots of God are twenty thousand, even thousands of angels: the Lord is among them..." Psalm 68:17

Silvery moonlight washed over the crude, two-story, wooden house. It was nine o'clock, and I was already asleep. Euni nestled deeper into her loveseat, trying unsuccessfully to concentrate on the notepad in her lap, on which were scrawled the first few lines of a letter to her parents. The darkness, the silence, and the thought of her parents so far away caused a wave of loneliness to wash over her.

The children were all asleep, and everything was quiet – too quiet. Euni blew out the candle and knelt beside the bed. *"Dear Father, I am afraid tonight. I know you care. Please watch over me and my precious family."*

Just across the ravine, perched high on a hill, another house glowed in the moonlight. Several young people sat out on the open porch, talking quietly and admiring the Nicaraguan mountains shimmering in the light of the near-full moon.

Suddenly Kiria (KEE ree ah) pointed toward our house in the valley. "What's that?"

"I was just going to ask the same thing!" Carmen exclaimed. They gazed in wonder at the glowing pillar of cloud hovering over the shed beside the house. "There's another one!" Carmen continued. "Back farther, a little to one side."

"They're angels!" Kiria announced breathlessly. "I can see their forms!" Kiria saw them plainly – outstretched wings, glowing legs, even a shining face turned toward our house. Goosebumps popped out all over their bodies. Was it, or wasn't it?

"They have to be at least twenty feet tall!" Edwin whispered in awe. "Look!" he said, pointing at the house again. "I see one on the lawn by the corner of the house. Can you see the glow?"

The girls couldn't see that one. For about five minutes they talked excitedly. They felt the angelic presence and the presence of God.

Suddenly the soft, cloudlike beings began to move, as if a wind were stirring. But there was no wind. Then the white glows disappeared. Though the watchers continued to search the darkness, they saw nothing more.

The next morning Carmen and Kiria came down to our house in the valley. As they burst in the door, Kiria was almost stammering with excitement. "Last night we saw angels over your house!" With tears in her eyes, she told us the story.

Angels over Waslala? Were they angels or not? Kiria was the most convinced. For her, it was a beautiful confirmation that God's angels were watching over us here in Waslala.

Carmen, always levelheaded and practical, was the most skeptical. She couldn't say she saw the angels' distinct forms. But she did say they tried their best, as they stood on the porch, to see if there could be some natural explanation. There was no fire or smoke. There were no low-hanging clouds, only lovely moonlight and two distinct, hovering glows, and possibly a third one in the distance. She admitted it was a beautiful experience.

After hearing Kiria's and Carmen's versions, I really wanted to talk to Edwin. I found his story right in between. There were definitely two, glowing *somethings* hovering over our home. The third wasn't nearly as clear. He also saw a form in the tallest cloud, but not distinctly the form of an angel. He remembered seeing legs. "We were excited," Edwin admitted. "Imagination could have played a part."

"Edwin," I asked, "I need to know exactly how you feel. Do you believe it was angels?" Edwin hesitated, so I added, "Did you believe it was angels last night?"

"Absolutely!"

"That's enough," I said. "If you felt they were real at the moment, I believe they were." I questioned them thoroughly, because I didn't want to write this story if it was just imagination. They thought I was skeptical. I wasn't. I just wanted to be sure.

"One thing is for sure, Pablo," Edwin continued. "Whether or not we saw angels, it was a beautiful experience, and I'm sure God used it to confirm His protection over us. And Pablo, think about it – we knew all along they were here, didn't we?"

"Amen, brother. We don't need to see them. But Edwin, I've always longed to. I believe God gave you a glimpse last night. I almost envy you."

"Don't envy me!" Edwin retorted. "You were the ones they were protecting! That's better than seeing."

He was right. Though we didn't see them, we were the ones for whom God had chosen to prove His protection – for me, my precious Euni and our children. That was better than seeing.

Later, talking with Euni and the children, we wondered, were there wicked men around right at the time? Were they planning a kidnapping? A rape? A killing? Did they perhaps come around the back, through the woods?

Let's just imagine a tiny bit more... Euni kneeling by her bed in the still of the night... armed men sneaking up behind the barn from the woods, single file... all of a sudden, God allows the spiritual beings to become visible. Imagine the frightened men turning and plunging back through the woods, sliding down over the steep bank, splashing through the creek, terrified of God's agents that protect His own. After the men leave, the angels again become invisible.

Could this be possible? Of course! It happened in Bible times. It can still happen today. Did it really happen that way? We don't know. But there is no doubt in our minds that there are many great and wonderful angels over Waslala.

After our visitors left, we gathered as a family and savored a precious moment together, thanking God for His protection. When we had been chosen by God and the Costa Rican churches to move to Waslala, we hadn't known it was one of the most dangerous places in Nicaragua. God hadn't wanted us to know. But He did want a shining testimony of His love in the dark mountains of Waslala.

And that's why He sent His bright, shining angels to protect us – visibly this once, invisibly always. This is their story – and His story – even more than ours. ❧

Pablo Yoder
Waslala, Nicaragua

Compiler's Note: The night when the youth saw the angels was Feb. 10, 1998. Pablo and his family still live in Waslala, Nicaragua, on a little farm with cattle, a garden, two pet monkeys and an alligator in a pond. They have lived in Waslala for twenty years, having moved there from Costa Rica in June, 1995. He writes books for a living, and pastors the Waslala Christian Brotherhood, a congregation of 48 members. Pablo and Euni have four married children, and two at home.

From *Angels in the Night* by Pablo Yoder. Used by permission.
© 2007 TGS International, PO Box 355, Berlin, Ohio 44610

Do Angels Have Names?

➤ Many angels and archangels are mentioned in the Bible. But only the names of two are given, in Luke 1:19 and Revelation 12:7. Who are they?

    G_____   M_____

➤ What man in the Bible wrestled all night with an angel? _____ (Genesis 32:24-29)

➤ What man in the Bible made broth for an angel? _____ (Judges 6:11-21)

9
Power on Her Head

"For this cause ought the woman to have power on her head because of the angels." 1 Corinthians 11:10

O ne summer day, in 2002, while we were living in Zanesville, Ohio, my husband, Crist, wanted to know if I would mind doing the banking. I decided I would go to the bank first before I did my other shopping.

The bank is not very busy right now, I thought, when I arrived. But I needed to stand in line for a while, because the few tellers they had were busy helping other customers.

While standing there, I noticed a young man come into the bank and walk just inside the doors. He stopped and looked around. I tried not to make it too obvious that I was watching, but something seemed to be amiss with him.

He proceeded further into the bank and stood in the line behind me. From where I was standing, I could see him on the side. He moved around a lot, went over to the wall desk and acted as if he was getting something. Yet, all the time I never saw anything in his hands.

While continuing to stand there, I could hear him mumbling something but was not sure what he was saying. I soon saw the tellers and another lady were watching also. Then I realized he was saying something to me.

He asked me what that thing was on my head. It was in a mocking tone, in a voice I was not sure about. The teller soon said she could help me. I was thankful to move forward. I was breathing a prayer all along, asking God for protection. The teller seemed to take her time helping me. I also noticed other people appearing behind the counter from somewhere else.

A couple of teller windows farther down, the other teller said she could help him. He walked up and asked if they could cash a check for him. The teller asked if he had an account with that bank.

"I asked, could you cash a check?" he very quickly replied. The teller proceeded to say there would be a charge if he did not have an account.

I noticed all eyes seemed to be turned that way, and a man stood behind the teller. The young man repeated the same thing again. Finally the teller asked if she could see the check. Up to this point, he had handed nothing to her.

I was soon done, and yet hesitated to walk behind the man to go out of the bank. But I proceeded to do so, and right after I got out the door, there he came after me! He came up rather close behind me and said, "That thing on your head kept me from doing what I wanted to do. There were angels all around you!"

I gave him a knowing look and quickly walked to my vehicle. He was talking loudly and crossed over to the next parking lot and drove away.

After getting into the van, I just sat there for a while. I was so weak, and I was trying to grasp what this man was up to. Thank the Lord for His protecting hand! I noticed the bank personnel were at the door watching.

After he drove away, I was sitting there for quite a while longer. I finally managed to get out of the van and talk to the bank personnel. They had heard him say something when he went out but couldn't understand him. They were very considerate and wanted to make sure I was alright and could make it home.

I had noticed he went the opposite way I was planning to go, so I felt safe to go home. The bank closed for a while that afternoon so the workers could calm down, as this incident created some anxiety among them.

Do we realize how much God's protecting hand is over us, keeping us from harm? It made me realize anew my dependence on God and the significance of the headship veiling I wear. *"For this cause ought the woman to have power on her head because of the angels" 1 Cor. 11:10.* The power on our heads is from God and it kept evil away that day. From what that man said, I often wondered what scene he saw. Though I had been somewhat nervous, I felt a calm protecting hand around me.

Friends, let's not lay this scripture aside – it is God's instruction in His Word. I realize that some Christian women have been disgraced while wearing a veiling, and yet I believe God honors the faithful observance of this New Testament teaching. My experience is not an isolated case. Do we, as Christian women, wear a head covering in joyful obedience to God, or do we wear it grudgingly? Its power to protect may be limited by the manner in which it is worn. ✍

Anna Byler, 2006
Canaan, NY

10

Triumph Over Evil

"The angel of the Lord encampeth round about them that fear Him, and delivereth them." Psalm 34:7

While visiting Haiti, in April, 1995, my daughter and I experienced the Lord's power and the certainty of the promises in His Word. We were part of a team that visited the staff of Christian Aid Ministries, ministering for a long weekend over Good Friday and Easter. The staff had informed us of the voodoo activity (devil worship) going on at that time of year.

A brother from CAM offered to take us on a tour of the capital, Port-au-Prince, in a pickup truck. As we went down the mountain and came around a bend and looked up ahead, we saw the road was packed with people from ditch to ditch – jumping, dancing, drinking, beating their drums and coming our way.

Immediately, the driver stopped the truck and put it in park. The fifty or sixty-yard gap was closing fast. A few of the women were dressed in bright yellow and red. We were told these were witches.

My 18-year-old daughter was with me on the back of the truck. We were watching with amazement, when all of a sudden we noticed that one witch, about two feet taller than the average height of the crowd, was floating back and forth from ditch to ditch, spinning 360° circles as she went. At that moment, a great fear gripped me and held me tight.

By then, the crowd of satanic worshippers was 25 yards from our pickup. Riveted with fear, I cried out to God for His protection.

Immediately, God gave me a verse in Psalm 34: *"The angel of the Lord encampeth round about them that fear Him, and delivereth them"* Psalm 34:7.

I quoted this verse out loud and told the Lord, *"Lord, I fear you. Please protect us."* Immediately, God's peace and calmness settled over the pickup like a canopy.

Right after this took place, another witch, who was carrying an umbrella, made eye contact with me. She was very demonic and evil-eyed. She came charging at me, not with human strength, but with satanic power – probably covering sixty feet in three or four jumps, basically flying through the air. She came right next to me and we were three feet apart, face-to-face.

With all the strength that Satan gave her, she tried to ram the end of her umbrella point between my eyes. But it stopped twelve inches from my forehead as if it had hit a glass wall. She pulled the umbrella back, and with all her power, she tried again – her target was between my eyes. Again, at twelve inches, she hit a glass wall. Very evil and determined, she tried the third time, with the same results.

Then she stopped and looked straight into my eyes. I did the same to her, and with a smile on my face I waved to her in perfect peace. Right after that, she gave up on me and took one huge, inhuman leap into the ditch and lay there like a bag of water, covered with sweat, and passed out.

By this time the crowd was past the truck and the driver started down the road again. I sat there, very humbled and grateful to be one of God's children, serving a Lord that is alive and always backs up His promises in the Bible. I was also very grateful that the Lord gave me the privilege of memorizing this verse so that it was there in a time of need. My daughter told me she had the same gripping fear that I had felt, and she also felt God's presence encamp around the truck.

Later on, as I relived that day, I wondered why this witch had picked me out since I was only one of six or eight people on the truck. I was no different from anyone else.

This is what the Lord showed me as I prayed over this experience: the power of the written Word of God that came from my lips clashed tremendously with her evil, demonic spirit. The two kingdoms were at war. (Psalm 119:89; Matthew 24:35; Psalm 138:2). I bless God for His protection that day, and I pray that His love will draw this poor woman to a new life in Him and set her free from Satan's bondage. ✍

Emanuel (Mannie) Troyer, 2015
Plains, MT

"For we wrestle not against flesh and blood, but against principalities, against powers, against the rulers of the darkness of this world, against spiritual wickedness in high places." Ephesians 6:12

11

Warrior Angels

"And David lifted up his eyes, and saw the angel of the Lord stand between the earth and the heaven, having a drawn sword in his hand…"

1 Chronicles 21:16

Part 1

There were few hints of the storms we would encounter as the *Sharon Singers* began to learn their songs in the winter of 2003 to 2004. Neither were there any indications of the miracles we would encounter in the midst of the brewing storms. Without warning, the squalls crashed in on us one night while our administrator, Val Yoder, was out of state for the founding board meeting of IGO, a new Bible school training center in Thailand.

In a coronary emergency, threatening to extinguish her life, Val's wife, Krystal, was airlifted to a series of hospitals. The same night, the choir director was hospitalized with chest pains. A week later, a biopsy confirmed cancer for him. Within hours, students and staff experienced a car accident, emergency surgery, and a second case of cancer was confirmed. There was also a near drowning and a stroke in the director's family.

A 24-hour prayer chain swung into effect as Krystal's life hung in the balance. As anguished students cried out to God during choir practice, one of them glimpsed warrior angels flying up through the ceiling, swords drawn as they headed westward at the moment that code blue was called on Krystal in the Johnstown, Pennsylvania, hospital.

Amazingly, before any of the storms had struck, our wise, all-knowing Father had given us the inspirational theme, *Peace in the Storm*. The songs touched us profoundly, gave us courage, strengthened us, and gave us vision and focus. In the storms of life, God not only gives us peace, but gives us an anchor for the soul as the mounting waves come crashing in. He has promised in Isaiah 26:3, *"Thou wilt keep him in perfect peace, whose mind is stayed on Thee; because he trusteth in Thee."*

Part 2

The following is Lanus Dueck's story during the previous events:

It is during the most difficult times in our journey that God reveals Himself in some special way to bring His people new strength and courage. It was during one of these times in my life that God met me in a special way. I want to share this experience, not because I think I deserve any special recognition, but because God deserves all the honor and praise that I, as a Christian, can give Him.

I came to SMBI (Sharon Mennonite Bible Institute) to learn more about God, and one of my prayers was that my faith in Him would grow. I had never dreamed that He would answer my prayer the way He did. Here is how it happened.

Monday, January 19, 2004, started out like any other day for me at school. But when I came out of my dorm, I heard that Krystal, our administrator's wife, had been airlifted to the Johnstown Hospital during the night, with congestive heart failure. Like everyone else at the school, I was shocked and started praying that God would be with the family and send healing, if it was His will.

Not knowing what the day would bring, I went to class with a heavy heart. Since I hadn't heard many of the details how things had unfolded during the night, I was thankful that our teacher gave us an update on Krystal's condition. We decided to skip the notes for the first part of class and just spend some time in prayer, seeking God's face.

We cleared all the desks and formed a circle, kneeling on the floor, and had a time of prayer, intercession and singing. It is hard to describe the many different feelings that came to me, including disbelief and desperation. But I think the most painful experience for me during this time was when the Spirit reminded me of Krystal's son, Daniel, who was in Thailand, and the feelings of helplessness he would be going through.

Around that time, I felt God telling me, this is *war*! And that Satan was intensely involved, fighting to take Krystal's life or health since that could seriously disrupt, or even destroy the family's plans to go to Thailand in a few years. So I felt a real need to pray, and fight against the powers of darkness, and ask God to show His power.

The entire student body went through a lot of emotional turmoil those days. Every mealtime, we would have an update. And a few times during class, we heard the intercom announcement to meet in the chapel immediately – we didn't know what to expect, and fear would grip my heart every time.

It seemed we were riding in a boat with one of the toughest storms in our lives raging on the outside. Lots of time was spent in prayer, asking God to send healing if it was His will.

On Wednesday, Jan. 21, during our afternoon choir practice, Cliff, our assistant administrator, walked into the chorus room, followed by the remainder of the staff and the students who were not already assembled there. The look on his face brought a painful silence over the entire choir. I thought Krystal had died and that all our prayers had been in vain.

Cliff told us that Marcus Yoder had just phoned from the hospital and told him "code blue" had been called for Krystal's room – her heart was failing and every available doctor and nurse had been summoned. Even though she hadn't died, her life was hanging in the balance, and we needed to cry out to God and beg Him for her life.

We were shocked! I wrestled with questions. *Why, God, after all our prayers and tears, is this it? She can't die! Why?*

Many of the students didn't need Cliff's urging to begin praying. As those around me started crying out to God, I was still questioning Him and couldn't believe that this was happening. Right then, a friend of mine, Josiah, put his arm around me and started praying. I had my eyes open and was looking around the room, watching the others praying, when I started my own little prayer.

Soon after I closed my eyes, I saw a vision of angel warriors popping out of the SMBI roof! It was as if each one was a direct response to a prayer. The warriors were already on the roof when another one appeared. It seemed that God was telling me, because I started praying later than the rest of the students, my angel was late. I saw one angel grabbing his sword, and to my amazement, they were all facing towards Johnstown! I had a sense that they took off for the hospital – where Krystal was fighting for her life – to combat the powers of darkness.

Along with the vision, although it was very short, the verse in Exodus 14:14 kept running through my mind: *"The LORD shall fight for you, and you shall hold your peace."* God was telling me that He was with us, and yes, He was fighting for us! After the vision, I felt very unworthy and had a special sense of peace in my heart that God was about to do something *big.*

The following weekend, I heard how much Krystal had improved, and that by Monday, the doctors were planning to let her walk. I was awed how God had really fought for us. My faith in Him had been small, even after the vision and the sense that He was about to do something big. I had still doubted Him.

But, praise God, He is patient with us even if our faith is small. Through this experience, my faith in God has greatly increased. I want to thank Him for all He has done and will continue to do. ❧

Urie Sharp, 2015
Bolivar, OH

❧ Compiler's Note: Urie Sharp was SMBI's music instructor and choir director for many years. Lanus Dueck is serving the Lord in Thailand as a missionary with IGO (*Institute for Global Opportunities*).

To him that overcomes the foe,
White raiment shall be given,
Before the angels he shall know
His name confessed in heaven.

Then onward from the hills of light,
Our hearts with love aflame,
We'll vanquish all the hosts of night
In Jesus' conquering name!

(Encamped Along the Hills of Light
– John Yates; Ira D. Sankey)

12

What a Night!

"And, behold, the angel of the Lord came upon him, and a light shined in the prison: and he smote Peter on the side, and raised him up, saying, 'Arise up quickly.' And his chains fell off from his hands." Acts 12:7

The Christian church was under attack. King Herod arrested some of the followers of Jesus, intending to persecute them, and ordered that James, the brother of John, be killed. Peter was his next target. After arresting him, King Herod made sure he was securely imprisoned. Peter was guarded by four squads of soldiers – a total of sixteen guards!

But King Herod did not know the God of might and power. The church prayed earnestly and unceasingly for Peter. The night before Herod planned to bring his prisoner out for a public trial, Peter fell asleep, bound with chains between two soldiers. More soldiers stood guard at the entrance.

Suddenly, in spite of all that security, an angel from God came in and a light shone in Peter's prison cell. The angel struck him gently at his side to wake him, and helped him get up.

"Get up quickly," the angel said, and the chains on Peter's hands fell off. "Put on your clothes and sandals. Wrap your cloak around you and follow me." Peter promptly obeyed and followed the angel.

They walked right past the guard at the entrance and on past the other guards. When they came to the large iron gate that led to the city, the gate opened and Peter and the angel walked right through!

Peter didn't know this all was real. He thought he was having a pleasant dream or seeing a vision. The angel and Peter walked down the street. All at once, Peter's guide left him. Peter was in a daze. What was happening? This was real! This was not a dream! Amazed and glorifying God for his deliverance, Peter said, *"Now I know of a surety, that the Lord hath sent His angel, and hath delivered me out of the hand of Herod, and from all the expectation of the people of the Jews"* (Acts 12:11).

Now, where should he go? After some consideration, he went to the house of Mary, where many had gathered for prayer. He knocked at the door of the gate. A servant girl named Rhoda went to answer. When she recognized Peter's voice, she was so overjoyed that she did not open the door, but ran back and told everyone that it was Peter who was knocking! They did not believe her, but said it was his angel. Peter continued knocking until they opened the door. He motioned for them to be quiet and told them about his angel experience and deliverance. He told them to tell the other believers, then left to go elsewhere.

In the morning, the king and the guards were greatly disturbed. Their prisoner was gone, and no one knew what had become of him! The guards were examined closely, and when Peter could not be found, they were executed.

But God was watching the evil behavior of King Herod, and sometime later, an angel of the Lord struck him down, and he died. What a God we serve! He is still the same today! ঌ

Vera Overholt, 2016
Sarasota, FL

ঌ Compiler's Note: Story adapted from Acts 12

Thoughts to Ponder

As you think about the previous story of Peter's deliverance:

- King Herod had Peter guarded *all around*, but he did not *look up* to the Lord, who watches and defends from above.

  No matter how strong an earthly power, God is always stronger! He hates injustice and loves to rescue the helpless (Psalm 18:1-19).

- King Herod's decisions were creating fear and anxiety among those he was responsible to protect and lead. But God was watching, and decisively judged his increasing arrogance.

  Evil authority causes insecurity, confusion, stress and chaos. It destroys trust, and scatters and drives away those in its care. In contrast, true authority is a continual and consistent source of life, safety, provision, blessing and encouragement, creating an environment where all can flourish (Jeremiah 23; Mt. 20:25-28). Which type of authority are you?

- Peter was sleeping in spite of desperate circumstances.

  Are the circumstances of your life causing you to feel anxious and fearful? Remember that your Father loves you, that He is powerful, and that He will never leave you! Like Peter, you can experience rest in the face of uncertainty (Philippians 4:6, 7).

- Peter thought his angelic rescue was all a dream.

  Peter and the other believers were as human as we are – they were all surprised when God answered their prayer. Do you carry an umbrella when you pray for rain? Or have you given up hope that God hears your prayers? Be assured that angels are helping you, too, even when you don't see them.

- Peter was delivered by the angel the night before his trial.

  God is with you, whether or not the prison doors swing open! He is never too late! (Joseph's years in prison prepared him to reign wisely). God loves you and delights in rescuing those that fear Him (Ps. 9:12; Ps. 10:17, 18).

- Abigail Berryman

13

God's Healing Touch

"...Who maketh His angels spirits, and His ministers a flame of fire." Heb. 1:7

The tragedy which took the life of my husband, Martin, happened on January 25, 1990. Martin and I were serving the Lord in Sturgis, Michigan, during that time, in the mission church called Christian Fellowship Center (CFC). Everybody loved Martin, and his sudden death was a shock to all of us. We were working with many non-Christians coming in off the street and also young believers who were struggling to grow in their faith. Many blamed the devil for Martin's death, and I was disappointed that the enemy was getting the credit. *Lord, there is joy in Heaven when the saints come home. Jesus, You hold the keys of life and death.*

But though I didn't blame the devil for what seemed like a senseless and untimely death, I was confused and angry at God. Not only was I dealing with the grief of losing Martin, but our son, Larry, was sitting in jail, not receiving proper care.

It was because of Larry's schizophrenia that the accident had happened. He was hallucinating and thought he saw an opossum and went outside with his bow and arrow. He had been a hunter before his mental illness diagnosis, and was normally very careful. But when he returned inside, the arrow slipped from his hand and hit Martin in the chest, just deep enough to puncture his main artery. Larry should have been admitted to a mental hospital following Martin's death, but the prosecutor was determined to prove that the accident was intentional and have him placed in a state prison.

Despite my pleadings and having provided detailed evidence of his mental illness, the prosecutor wouldn't budge. Meanwhile, Larry was sitting confused and alone in the Centreville jail, not receiving the right medication. He would call me sometimes during the night and ask, "Why am I here, what happened?" He had no memory of the accident. (Growing up, Larry was a smart, healthy child with a high IQ, but when he was around 21, we saw that something was wrong. We were devastated when he was diagnosed with Schizophrenia, a serious mental disorder that distorts a person's thoughts, behaviors, perceived reality, and how they express emotions and relate to others).

It was now four weeks after Martin died, and I was struggling hard with God. One Sunday afternoon, I was driving alone on my way to see Larry, going west on M-86. I was hurting and crying, and screaming out loud to God. *Why is Larry sick? Why did this happen to Martin? Why? Why? Why?*

All at once, I felt a wonderful presence in my car, like somebody embracing me and comforting me. It was so real and so precious – words cannot express it. God's loving supernatural presence was so tangible, and I knew I was not alone in the car. Then I heard a gentle voice in my ear, saying, *"I want the glory from what took place."*

I knew the loving voice was God's voice, and I slowed the car down and yelled out, "God, from now on, You will get it!" Awe filled me and I felt overwhelmed by the unmistakable presence of God, bringing healing to my shattered heart and taking away my anger. I felt the angels with me even though I couldn't see them. They showed me it was Martin's time to go to heaven.

I never felt angry again, and I accepted the tragic losses in my life. I shared what had happened with my congregation and praised

God over and over for that wonderful experience. He met with me that day and comforted me, and healed my hurting heart from the pain, confusion and anger that was consuming me.

It wasn't until November that Larry had a court date. The judge immediately ruled that he was to be moved from jail to a mental hospital. It took Martin's death for Larry to get to where he is today – receiving the help and supervision he needs for his condition. I think Martin would be thankful, too, as he often felt sorry for Larry and was worried about what would happen to him when we could no longer take care of him.

Thank you, Jesus. He loves us. He cares about our pain and circumstances. He is waiting to heal our broken hearts when we cry out in desperation to Him. And He wants the glory for everything that happens in our lives, because what Satan intends for evil, God will *always* turn into something good. ᴥ

Mary Keely, 2016
Sturgis, MI

ᴥ Author's Note: I share this story to glorify the name of Jesus Christ, the One who is Almighty. *"And we know that all things work together for good to them that love God…" Romans 8:28.* All of life's circumstances, even the tragedies, work together for good. Praise His name. Another great promise for those who fear God is Proverbs 3:6, *"In all thy ways acknowledge Him and He shall direct thy paths."* May each one who reads this story be blessed as you serve the Lord faithfully.

14
Jesus Cares!

"And the angel of the LORD found her by a fountain of water in the wilderness... And the angel of the LORD said unto her, 'the LORD hath heard thy affliction.' And she called the name of the LORD that spake unto her, 'Thou God seest me.'" Genesis 16:7, 11, 13

My heart was feeling weary and heavy as I sat waiting at the Detroit Greyhound station. It was evening, and a wide variety of people were milling about.

It was August 2004, and I was spending several weeks at Deeper Life Ministries, in Ohio. I was working through painful issues in my life. I longed for freedom, yet Satan's forces felt strong.

I was traveling home to Fremont, Michigan, to attend a wedding, with plans to return to Deeper Life for further help. As I sat alone at the bus station, darkness wanted to close in. All around me were the evils of a wicked city. Inside me was the raging of a spiritual battle.

Suddenly, a young man stood in front of me. He looked very young, like a teenager, and his skin was pale white. He had such clear, blue eyes.

With a voice intense with emotion, he said, "I want you to know that today I am praying for you and your family." And then he left and returned to the crowd of travelers.

My heart was deeply touched, and I knew that God cared. I felt He had sent a ministering angel to encourage me at a low point in my life. Praise the Lord. He cares! And His love reaches to our deepest needs. ❧

Ida Mae Gascho
Fremont, MI

15

Springs in the Valley

"Blessed is the man whose strength is in You, whose heart is set on pilgrimage. As they pass through the Valley of Baca, they make it a spring... They go from strength to strength. Each one appears before God in Zion." Psalm 84:5-7 (NKJV). "And the angel said unto her, 'Fear not.'" Luke 1:30

When I lost my identical twin sister, Leora, nine years ago, I was unprepared for the tidal wave of grief that would consume me. It felt like half of me was gone. We had the kind of close-knit relationship that many sisters take for granted, talking on the phone two or three times a day. Because of our close bond, it also intensified the pain when a conflict arose between us – sometimes I unintentionally hurt her with my words and had to make it right. After Leora died, I pled with God, *"Please take me, too, I can't live on without my sister."* My husband, Nelson, was a comfort to me, but the pain of my loss seemed unbearable and I didn't know how I could go on.

But the Spirit of God gently spoke to me, *"I'm not finished with you. I want you to bring encouragement to Christians, starting with the little children in your congregation. Just put your hand on a child's head and say, 'I love you, and so does Jesus.'"* One Sunday morning, God showed me the first little girl that He wanted me to encourage. *"This is the girl."* So every Sunday, I placed my hand on her head and told her, *"I love you, and so does Jesus,"* and took an interest in her.

One Sunday, she timidly handed me a little sheet of paper. *"Thank you, Leona, for encouraging me,"* the note read.

That led to encouraging other young children, then adolescents, then young people and young mothers. It gave me purpose to reach out to others in the midst of my own grief. I also began passing out encouragement cards to people I didn't know, when I went shopping or into town for any reason.

I was struggling hard to go on purposefully with life and survive the loss of my twin sister when another wave of sorrow hit me two years later, and my only remaining sister, Anna Mae, died. The valley of sorrow through which I was walking seemed unending. Few people knew the depth of grief I was carrying deep inside, and it was hard for me to share it with others. It seemed no one could fully understand the *Valley of Baca* through which I was walking.

Around that time, I was going through another personal trial, and for three days, I wept, and cried out to God. On the third night, I tossed and turned and couldn't sleep. Finally, around midnight, I told my husband that I was going out to the living room.

As I walked to the loveseat, where I usually sat to have my quiet times with the Lord, the Spirit of God spoke to me. *"Remember Job? He lost all of his children, and his wife told him God didn't love him and he should curse God and die. And what did Job do? He gave a sacrifice of thanksgiving. He thanked God."*

Humbled by that reminder, I raised my hands and began praising God. For at least half an hour, I kept thanking Him and sensed His presence. Suddenly, I realized I was no longer alone in the living room. The Spirit of God quietly spoke into my mind, *"The person that is in the living room with you is a celestial being from heaven."* I looked around the dimly-lit room, and there, five feet from where I was sitting, was an angel dressed in white. I didn't feel any fear.

For half an hour, I continued praising God, in spite of my anguished heart. I knew the angel was there but didn't look again. Suddenly my arms felt heavy – like they had been in shackles from this trial – and just as quickly, the heaviness was lifted and my arms were released from the heavy chains. When that happened, the burden I was carrying was completely gone and I was free! I had experienced the amazing power of offering a sacrifice of praise in the midst of a trial.

I was so focused on praising God that I didn't see when the angel left. When I returned to the bedroom, Nelson was still awake. I couldn't contain my joy. *"I have been in the presence of God... I have seen an angel... I have the victory... I'm no longer in the mire of discouragement... the heavy burden is gone!"* Nelson praised God with me and we thanked Him for revealing Himself in such a special way, lifting my burden, and allowing me to see the angel.

That burden never came back. Like David experienced in the Valley of Baca, there were springs after that valley, springs of joy in the Holy Spirit. These verses became very real to us: *"Rejoice evermore. Pray without ceasing. In everything give thanks: for this is the will of God in Christ Jesus concerning you."* 1 Thessalonians 5:16-18.

As I reflect on the valleys I have walked through in recent years, here are some things I have learned:

- *Praise!* The power of God is mighty through praise and worship. Satan cannot stand praise. He's booted out, he's defeated, he's gone! When the devil comes and tries to bring discouragement, tell him, "Be gone, get out of this house," and lift up your hands and praise God.
- *Worship!* When you go through severe trials, worship God. Thank God. It is a powerful weapon against the enemy and releases the power of God to bring healing and freedom. Now, when I experience testing in my inter-personal

relationships, I have learned to worship God. I say out loud, "Praise God! Thank you, Jesus."

- *Sing!* Sing songs of redemption and thank God for the blood of Jesus. That is what gives us the victory. Satan tries to make us believe that we have not been redeemed. He is a liar. The Holy Spirit gives us the assurance of the presence of God and strengthens us. I'm not perfect either, and have made many mistakes, but God has forgiven me, as He will forgive you.

- *Pray!* You don't need polished prayers, just talk to Him as you would to a friend. God wants us to come to Him as a child and wants our relationship with Him to be trusting and uncomplicated. When we ask Him to be our Savior and Lord, His Spirit resides in our spirit, bringing peace and comfort and strength for whatever we may be facing.

- *Encourage!* Every day, make a commitment to the Lord that you want to make a difference in somebody's life that would draw them closer to God. Before I go anywhere, I pray that I can encourage someone that I meet. It's so easy to be in a hurry and overlook the people that God puts in our path each day.

As I reach out to bless others, and pass out my encouragement cards, God brings joy in the midst of sorrow, encouraging me in return. "I still have your card. Thank you for encouraging me," I hear, as I walk into Walmart. "I still have the card you gave me. It means so much to me," the manager of a restaurant said recently, when we walked in. "Thank you for praying for me," said the lady on the telephone, who called to thank me for the card I had given her when she was going through cancer treatment a couple of years earlier. She and her husband ended up coming to our home for a meal, and we were mutually encouraged.

One day, I had just finished eating at Wendy's, when the Lord brought a family to my attention, sitting at a nearby table. I sensed in my heart that they needed to talk. So, I walked over to the table where the man and his wife and two children were sitting and gave them my encouragement card, and began sharing my testimony how God had lifted me out of deep sorrow. I told them that God loves them. Sometime later, Nelson met the woman, Carol, in town. She told him she had planned to end her life the day that I had spoken with them at Wendy's. But because I had encouraged her, she didn't follow through with her plan of suicide. Nelson and I invited them to our home for supper, and they told us how much it meant to have friends, after having no friends. I stay in contact with Carol, and today, she is a changed lady and is doing well.

My dear friends, if you are at a very low point in your life, I know the feeling. Jesus met me at my lowest point and that is the reason I share my story. Jesus knows our sorrows. If you need a friend, cry out to God! God will hear your prayer. God loves you!

On another occasion, I was talking to a man I had met, and asked him what he thinks of this chaotic world we're living in. He readily answered, "I'm scared to death!" There are many people like him, who don't have the hope of salvation to carry them through the tough times. I like to tell them, "Don't fear tomorrow, God is already there."

And so we go *from strength to strength* in this pilgrimage of life, looking forward to heaven where there will be no more sorrow or parting or tears. *"They go from strength to strength. Each one appears before God in Zion."* Psalm 84:5-7 (NKJV). I pray that I will meet you there! ᥊

Leona Kurtz, 2016
Hartwell, GA

Some of the words on the encouragement card that Leona passes out:

I trust you, Jesus, in response to whatever happens to me today.
"Thou wilt keep him in perfect peace whose mind is stayed
on Thee: because he trusteth in Thee." Isaiah 26:3

16

"Yes, Lord!"

"And there appeared an angel unto him from heaven, strengthening him."

Luke 22:43

M y father and mother sold produce at many of the livestock auctions in Holmes, Tuscarawas and Wayne Counties, in Ohio.

There were five of us children, and we grew up in playpens, watching our parents work, but as soon as we were old enough, we helped sell watermelons and cantaloupes and passed out samples to potential customers. Father would say, "If you put a sample in a person's hand, it will help them to make a decision, so don't ask them if they *want* a sample, just place the sample in their hand."

Father would drive many hours in his old semi-truck to pick up a load of watermelons from Blackville, South Carolina, or Cordele, Georgia, or Immokalee, Florida, depending on what was in season.

So, picture with me this middle-aged man who is tired from hours of travel to and from Florida. His hair is slightly greasy from the lack of a shower, his beard – at one time black – is turning shades of salt and pepper, and he's been singing and praying and asking God to help him have a safe trip and to bless his family back home. He has hopes of selling this load of 2,000 watermelons and making some much-needed cash.

It's getting late, and he is becoming very tired. He's driving Interstate 77 north, and if he can make it to the top of Fancy Gap, he tells himself he's going to pull off and get some sleep. Fancy Gap is seven miles inside of Virginia, and the Blue Ridge Parkway goes through it. It's a steep, grueling mountain climb for an old truck and flatbed trailer like Father has. And downhill is even more dangerous, with 40,000 pounds of weight pushing him downward.

He shifts down one gear, two gears, three gears and more. The old International's four-ways are flashing, the engine groans, until he's barely crawling up that mountain road. At last he's reached the crest and the turnoff for the scenic overlook comes into view.

Sleep is near. He sets the emergency brake, kills the engine and slowly crawls into the sleeper. It's the end of May, and he's hoping to get these melons home for Memorial Day weekend. Sales will be brisk as people buy that first watermelon of the season for their picnics and family reunions. He breathes a word of prayer and drops off into an exhausted sleep, snoring loudly.

Suddenly, with a start, he wakens. The morning light of dawn is filtering into the cab of the truck, and it's very cold. Father crawls out of the sleeper and everything around is white with frost. He opens the door, climbs out of the cab and steps on a tire to crawl up onto the trailer.

As he clutches those blue four-foot sideboards, a horrible site meets his gaze. His 2,000 Crimson Sweet watermelons, hand-loaded and packed on fresh straw, have slumped down into misshapen, grotesque blobs of watery goo.

While he slept, there had been a freak, hard freeze. What do you think was going through his mind? His investment, scraped together, was gone! The fuel to Florida and back, used up!

What was he going to tell his wife? What would his children eat? I'm getting tears in my eyes as I'm relating this story, because it is painful. Bad things happen to all of us. How are we going to respond to them?

Suddenly, Father hears the sounds of a voice, and, glancing over, he sees a man approaching him, walking briskly across the gravel parking lot. He's calling out to Father, at the top of his voice, *"Yeeess, Looord," "Yeeess, Looord!" "Yeeess, Looord!"*

In telling this story, Father felt that God had sent this man, possibly an angel, to encourage him at that moment of decision. How would he respond? Would he thank God? Would he say, *"Not my will, but Yours be done"*? Many times Father told this story to congregations where he preached, and then he would ask them to repeat the words with him: *"Yes, Lord!"*

So, how are *you* responding to the bad things in your life? Are they making you bitter or are they making you better? The Holy Spirit would like to help you to make the right decision today. Now, let's repeat these words together: "YES, LORD!" ⟞

Nathan Overholt, 2010
Sarasota, FL

⟞ Compiler's Note: As my son, Nathan, recalls, my husband often used this story from the pulpit to encourage others to say "yes" to the Lord and not to become bitter about life's circumstances. My daughter, Sarah, remembers the following details: "As Father stood there, dejected, the man kept loudly repeating 'Yeeess, Laaawd,' 'Yeeess, Laaawd,' in his southern drawl, until Father joined in repeating it with him. As he continued to say those words, peace entered his heart and he came to a place of surrender and acceptance of God's will. As he looked at his load and continued repeating these words, the man walked away. Father turned to talk to him, and he was nowhere to be seen! This is why Father, later, would ask congregations to repeat with him several times, 'Yes, Lord,' to say the words *out loud* even though they didn't feel like it, to make a conscious, verbal choice of surrender to the Lord's will, in the face of their losses."

17

The Scissors Sharpener

*"And there came an angel of the Lord, and sat under an oak...and said...
'The Lord is with thee...'" Judges 6:11, 12*

One very cool, spring morning, when I was living in Lancaster County, Pennsylvania, I was attempting to hang out the wash. But I was in a wrestling match with the wind which was whipping the clothes every which way.

As I worked, I began singing "In the Sweet By and By." All at once, a little, old man with a satchel in one hand was standing beside me and said, "I haven't heard anyone sing that song like that for a long time."

I asked the stranger, "Have you had breakfast? Please go in through the sun parlor, first door to the left, and sit by the stove and warm yourself." I noticed he looked really cold in his threadbare coat.

Before going into the house, my visitor asked me if I had scissors that needed sharpening. "Yes, I surely do," I told him.

After I was finished hanging out the load of wash, I prepared breakfast for him. I noticed he silently returned thanks before he ate.

While he was eating, I hung out more wash, and then went back into the kitchen again. When the stranger had finished his breakfast, he stood. Facing me, he placed his hands on my shoulders and said, "May the God of Abraham, Isaac and Jacob guide and keep you all the days of your life."

As he gently touched my shoulders, it seemed like an electrical shock went through me from head to foot. For a few seconds, I could not move at all, not even my eyes. With him standing before me, I noticed his perfect cleanliness and his beautiful, blue eyes. I completely forgot about the scissors sharpening.

A few minutes later, while hanging out the last load of wash, I saw my visitor standing in the middle of the crossroad by our home, looking up into the sky with his hands crossed above his head. I did not see his satchel.

The following day, at our church service, I inquired of our nearby neighbor families if they had also seen the scissors sharpener. But no one had seen him.

Could this have been an angel? My life has not been the same since. The Lord has become more precious to me. ❧

Amanda Zook
Gap Mills, WV

"Though I speak with the tongues
(languages) of men and of angels,
and have not charity,
I am become as sounding brass,
or a tinkling cymbal."

1 Corinthians 13:1

18

The Tramp

"Be not forgetful to entertain strangers: for thereby some have entertained angels unawares." Hebrews 13:2

This is a story that happened to me when I was a little girl. I come from a large family of 11 children – four boys and seven girls. We lived on top of a hill in a big, brown farmhouse.

My sister, Rachel, was the youngest in the family and I was next to Rachel. We were great pals. We loved to go upstairs in the barn and climb up the ladders to the loft and look for baby kittens, or jump in the hay that my father stored up there.

One day, when we were playing in the loft, I looked out the little window. I could see way down the road to our neighbor's place, around a mile or more away. Suddenly, I saw someone come walking up the road. It was a tramp! I could tell it was a tramp by the shaggy, old clothes he wore and the bag he carried on his back.

"Let's quickly run to the house," I said to Rachel, "a tramp is coming." I was kind of afraid of the tramps. They never did anything bad to us, but they looked so rough, with whiskers all over their faces. We called them *tramps* because they walked from place to place and asked for food. Many tramps were homeless and poor. Back in those days you would often see them, and they always had their places they would stop for food. Our place was one of them. My mother was so kind, and the tramps must have known she would never turn them away.

Rachel and I ran inside. Soon we heard the tramp knocking on the door. My mother opened the door and said a cheery, "Hello."

"Could I have something to eat, Ma'am?" he asked.

"Yes, just have a seat on the steps there, and I'll get you something," said Mother. Soon Mother had some good left-overs heated and a nice, big plate of food ready. We tried to peep out and watch him.

After a while, he was done eating. Usually, tramps left when they finished eating. But this time, he asked, "May I sleep in your barn tonight?" Oh, dear, I didn't want mother to say *yes*! I had heard from other children that sometimes tramps would burn your barn down while everyone was sleeping.

Mother asked someone to go to the barn and get my father. They talked about it for a little while, and then Father told him: "Yes, you may sleep here tonight. But instead of sleeping in the barn, you may sleep in our summer house, upstairs. It will be more comfortable there."

Oh, no, I didn't want the tramp to sleep at our house! I was so afraid. That night, I really prayed. *God, please protect us, and please don't let the tramp burn our house down.* The next morning I awoke, and everything was fine. Our house wasn't burned down, and everyone was safe.

"Come down for breakfast," called Mother. I came running down the steps and ran into the kitchen. Guess who was sitting at the kitchen table? The tramp! We all took our places around the table, and Father asked the blessing. I'm sure I peeped during prayer to see if the tramp was praying.

After breakfast, the tramp got up to leave. He thanked us for the good food and bed. Then he picked up his bag, slung it over his shoulder and went out the door.

Soon after he left, I went to the window to watch him go, but he was nowhere to be seen! I looked down one direction, but he wasn't there. I looked the other way, but he wasn't there either! That puzzled me for a long time.

Years later, when I was older, I read a verse in the Bible that made me wonder (Hebrews 13:2). Could that tramp have been an angel? Did God want to test us to see if we would be kind and feed the man and let him sleep at our house? It could be. 1 Peter 4:9 reminds us to *"use hospitality one to another without grudging."*

Two things I want you to remember about this true story. Always show kindness, no matter who the person is. And when you're afraid, always pray. God hears you. He has angels that watch over you and protect you. ✍

Ruby Sommers Miller, 2006
Canton, OH

❧ Compiler's Note: My younger sister, Ruby, lives with her husband, Aden, near Hartville, Ohio. They have three children and 13 grandchildren.

Food for Thought

➤ What does the Bible say is the food of angels? M_____ (Psalm 78:24, 25)

Meeting Angels Unaware

On life's busy thoroughfare,
We meet with angels unaware,
But we are too busy to see or hear,
Too busy to sense that God is near.

Too busy to stop and recognize
The grief that lies in another's eyes.
Too busy to offer to help or share,
Too busy to sympathize or care.

Too busy to do the good things we should,
Telling ourselves we would if we could.
But life is too swift and the pace is too great,
And we dare not pause for we might be late,
For our next appointment which means so much,
We are willing to brush off the Saviour's touch.

And we tell ourselves there will come a day,
We will have more time to pause on our way.
But before we know it, life's sun has set,
And we've passed the Saviour, but never met.

For hurrying along life's thoroughfare,
We passed Him by and remained unaware
That within the very sight of our eye,
Unnoticed, the Son of God passed by.

~ Helen Steiner Rice

19

A Bold Request

"Let us therefore come boldly unto the throne of grace, that we may obtain mercy and find grace to help in time of need." Hebrews 4:16
"Who is gone into heaven, and is on the right hand of God; angels and authorities and powers being made subject unto Him." 1 Peter 3:22

Early in life, I was led by the Spirit to devote my entire time to the work of the ministry. By the grace of God, I sought to live strictly by faith. An encouraging twelve months' trial continued for the rest of my long, active life in almost unbroken succession.

Confiding my needs solely to the Father, and taking up no collections, I literally lived from meal to meal and from day to day. While traveling in gospel interests, I started six different times for the railway depot without money, knowing God would supply the necessary cash in some manner, and not once was I disappointed.

On one occasion, I was planning to leave the following day from a camp meeting, for an appointment hundreds of miles distant. I experienced such a realization of the presence of God that I was emboldened to ask Him for a special favor. I prayed that the means for a railway ticket would be withheld until it was actually needed, and expressed to the Lord a wish that the money might reach me through some unusual channel. I just wanted to witness a greater manifestation of His power and glory.

No one thereabouts knew me. No one knew of my plan. No one knew I was penniless. When the time of departure arrived, I was a little late and was running to catch a train that was already slowly pulling out of an outlying country station, far from my personal contacts.

Suddenly, a perfect stranger appeared in the way, accosted me, grabbed my hand, and thrust into it a wad of paper money and some silver. I had never seen or heard of him before, nor have I seen or heard of him since. The money, to a cent, paid my railroad fare to the city whereto I was bound!

Could it be that my gracious messenger was a supernatural being, heaven sent? And had I been so singly honored for but one fleeting moment, as to have been brought face to face with an angel? I wonder! ❧

Brother Charles

❧ Pilgrim Tract Society. Used by permission.

20

Bill, the Hitchhiker

"Behold, I send an Angel before thee, to keep thee in the way..." Ex. 23:20

I t was late fall, 1990, and our family had just returned to Florida after four weeks of nightly singing and ministering in congregations across the United States. This was preceded by four weeks of travel in Western and Eastern Europe, participating in open-air meetings, singing and preaching in congregations, and personal interactions on trains as we traveled.

I was exhausted both physically and mentally and was ready to resume working and getting back to a normal schedule instead of living out of a suitcase. The van we had rented in Lancaster, Pennsylvania, for our stateside traveling, now needed to be returned to the rental company.

As soon as we unloaded, I cleaned out the van and repacked my suitcase and headed north on Interstate 75. I had asked a friend, Jon, to go along with me and keep me company, and the miles passed as we visited and told stories. North of Ocala, we crossed over to Route 301, and then picked up Interstate 95, north of Jacksonville, making good time.

Somewhere in South Carolina, I saw a man standing on the shoulder of the highway. I braked hard, swerved over onto the rumble strip, and then backed the van to the hitchhiker, who had started walking towards us. Jon rolled down the window.

"Where are you going?" I asked.

"Richmond, Virginia," he replied.

"Well, we're going past there. Get in!" He climbed into the passenger front seat as Jon moved back to a middle seat. He was a black man, around sixty years old, well dressed, but not flashy. He was serious, not overly talkative, but willing to converse.

Bill told us he had enjoyed working as a bus driver for Greyhound but had recently retired after a lengthy career. Now, he transported vehicles for a company, traveling around the country, picking up and delivering them. It was a less demanding job – solo trips – compared to the stressful piloting of large buses with passengers to care for. Often, his passengers had been cantankerous, partially inebriated, and just plain needy. At times, he had even found it necessary to call ahead and have police ready at the next stop to take someone off the bus. Bill spoke softly, but with depth and conviction that conveyed a feeling of peace, a self-assurance – a man who was comfortable in his own skin.

Somewhere in North Carolina, I began to grow tired, so tired that I just *had* to sleep. For some strange reason, instead of asking Jon to drive, which I had intended to do all along, I had a gut feeling that I should ask Bill. Bill agreed to drive and we pulled off at a truck stop and fueled up. I crawled into the back of the van and immediately fell asleep.

Hours later, I awoke with a start and sat up. Something was different. I peered over the seat and saw that it was evening, snowing hard, and we were driving slowly. Jon was fast asleep in the front, passenger seat, so I quietly eased towards the front and sat in the middle, behind Bill, where I could see the road.

I didn't say a word to Bill, but breathlessly observed, on pins and needles, my heart pounding. The interstate was glare ice on this stretch of I-95, and all around us, cars were spinning and sliding onto the shoulder and into the ditch. But Bill had a steady hand. I watched in amazement as he calmly drove on, firmly, resolutely, mile after mile up the highway.

The snow poured down, deeper, thicker. Visibility was poor, but on and on we went, closer to Richmond. It was dark now, and the red tail lights of other vehicles strained our eyes as we squinted through the windshield, partially blinded by the snow glaring off our headlights. The ice wasn't as bad now – that was good. But the snow was really coming down.

The lights of Richmond were finally in sight. Bill drove us to an upscale motel where he was planning to spend the night and meet his contacts. We shook hands and I gratefully thanked him for driving us through the treacherous ice.

We got back on the highway and headed north, and by the time we reached York, Pennsylvania, the road was blanketed in eight inches of snow. Tightly gripping the steering wheel, we crept slowly along, peering into the blinding, white, falling snow illuminated by our headlights. We followed an almost obscure set of windblown, tire tracks.

What a relief when we safely arrived in the wee hours of the morning at our friends' house near Lancaster, where we crawled into beds and sank into blessed sleep.

Over the years, as I have pondered this experience, I think God was smiling when we picked up this hitchhiker along the road. I, the "do-gooder," was trying to help someone in need, wanting to show kindness and compassion to a stranger. But the needy man turned into the giver, and I became the recipient! Straight from Florida's snow-free climate, tired from months of strenuous traveling, making a fast round-trip to Pennsylvania to return the van and hurry home to work and normal life, *I* was the needy man and didn't realize it, and the *feared hitchhiker* ended up helping *me*. How ironic. How wonderful!

How do we know when to trust our visceral feelings when it flies in the face of protocol and culture? Why should I have trusted this man over my own or Jon's driving skills?

I believe in angels – ministering spirits sent out – good angels against evil angels, one army against another, fighting all-out battles for the souls of God's children.

Whether or not Bill was an angel in disguise, I don't know. But I *do* know that he was used by God to protect us on that hazardous, snowy evening. ❧

Nathan Overholt, 2016
Sarasota, FL

21

God Loves His Children

"Behold, mine Angel shall go before thee..." Exodus 32:34

D oes God reveal Himself to His children today as He did in days of yore? I will let you judge after I tell you my experience.

Joshua 1:9 gives us this promise, *"Be strong and of a good courage; be not afraid, neither be thou dismayed: for the Lord thy God is with thee whithersoever thou goest."*

Let me tell you about a miraculous experience for the glory of God the Father and the Lord Jesus Christ that inspired me to trust Him more. Even in the mundane things of life, He wants us to know that He cares for us even when we are unaware of our needs. The spine-tingler I want to tell you happened on Dec. 1, 2005.

On the evening before, Jake Coblentz called me and wondered if I would be able to pick up someone the next day at the Phoenix airport, at 10:16 a.m. He was not feeling well and felt it best to ask someone else to substitute for him, which I consented to do. He gave me the flight information, America West #280, from Columbus, Ohio.

Thursday morning, I left the house later than I meant to. America West uses Terminal 4 for their departures and arrivals. So, I parked our van on Level 4 of the seven-level parking garage. The couple I was to pick up was expecting to be met at the baggage claim.

I took the elevator to that level and began walking toward the carousels to find my party waiting for someone to assist them with their luggage, when I met a kind, mannerly airport employee who asked me if he could help me. I told him I was but a "taxi" driver and had come to pick up a couple who was to come in on flight #280 from Columbus. I also told him that the monitor showed that the plane had already arrived, so I would go and see if I could find them.

I went on toward the carousel where a crowd was gathering to wait for their luggage. Suddenly, over the intercom, I heard, "Jonas, meet your party at Door No. 2 at the baggage claim level."

I wasn't quite sure I had heard right, so I kept on walking and looking at the carousel monitors to see if I was heading to the right place for Flight #280. Then I heard it again, "Jonas, meet your party at Door No. 2 at the baggage claim level."

I had been looking for Door No. 2 just beyond the car rental desks and couldn't figure out where that door was. But by then I had decided that I must not have gone far enough. So I decided to go outside, where I was sure to find that door.

I went out through Door No. 6 and checked which direction to find Door No. 2. I hurried toward it and as I did, the announcement came the third time. This time the noise level was improved so I heard it more clearly: "Jonas, meet your party at Door No. 2, at the baggage claim level."

I then hurried down the sidewalk till I came to Door No. 2 and went inside. Immediately, I saw a couple at the lost-baggage-claim counter. I walked up to them and introduced myself. It was the couple I was looking for. I told them I was glad they had paged me over the intercom to direct me to where they were searching for their luggage.

They astounded me by saying, "We didn't page you on the intercom. We didn't even know that you would be picking us up."

I just looked at them and said, "This sounds like something the Lord would do for us, knowing that I would not be able to find you in the carousel area." I think the man I had met, who asked if he could assist me, was an angel in disguise as an airport employee, for I had not even given him my name at all. It seemed so unusual to hear a message come over the intercom using the first name only. I have no work shirt or jacket with my name on it, so I couldn't have been giving him my name that way.

We have an awesome God who always knows our whereabouts and also promised us in Hebrews 13:5-6, that He would take care of us: "*... For He hath said, I will never leave thee nor forsake thee. So that we may boldly say, the Lord is my helper, and I will not fear what man shall do unto me.*" Amen!

The lost luggage was soon found and we went on our way to Ash Court to enjoy the beautiful sunshine in the Valley of the Sun. Praise His name! He cares for us! ⤳

Jonas Hershberger, 2007
Huntsburg, OH/Phoenix, AZ

22

My First Flight Alone

"Praise ye Him, all His angels: praise ye Him, all His hosts." Ps. 148:2
"Thou art worthy, O Lord, to receive glory, honor and power..." Rev. 4:11

It was Tuesday morning, Oct. 12, 2010. My son, Matthew, came at 4:45 a.m., and loaded my suitcase and carry-on bag into the car and we headed for Greensboro Airport. We were living in North Carolina at that time, and it was the first time I was flying by myself. I had always depended on my husband to guide me through the maze at airports.

My son went into the airport and stayed with me until I had checked in to go through security. *"Lord, be with me and help me to be a light in this dark and evil world,"* I prayed. This was good for me, because I prayed a lot more since I was traveling by myself.

I went through security and found my United Airlines departure gate to O'Hare, the huge airport in Chicago. The Bible verse came to my mind, *"Be strong and of good courage, fear not, nor be afraid of them; for the LORD thy God, He it is who doth go with thee"* (Deut. 31:6).

The weather was beautiful and we had a wonderful flight, floating through the fluffy clouds to Chicago. *Thank you, Lord!* But getting off the airplane and being with crowds of people was something else.

"Where do I go to fly to Sioux Falls?" I asked an agent.

"Go down the hall to F-12, down the stairs and onto a bus to another building and concourse."

I picked up my luggage and was walking with throngs of people, some walking very fast and some running. I started to pray, "*Lord, I really don't know where to go. I'm all by myself, and scared. Please show me where to go!*"

As I was praying out loud, a lady was walking beside me. I looked over and said, "Ma'am, I'm flying to Sioux Falls. Would you have any idea where I go from here?"

A kind gentleman stepped out from behind me and said, "Follow me. I know where to take you!" He carried my suitcase and we went downstairs and outside and got on a shuttle bus. My guide was very gracious and kind and stayed with me all the while. We soon arrived at the other concourse building where I needed to go, and we walked a distance together to my departure gate. "Here is where you fly to Sioux Falls," he said.

Thank you, Lord. Wow! You are so good. I looked up at the monitor, making sure the flight was the right one. The departure time was 10:50 a.m. I turned around to thank this kind gentleman for helping me, but he was gone! *Oh, God! I wanted to thank this gentleman. Please bless him wherever he goes today!* I walked around a little, hoping to find him. A lot of people were coming and going, and I couldn't really remember what he looked like. But I didn't see him anymore.

I was so awed by God's quick response to my plea. All of a sudden, a thought struck me. *This was God's angel! God takes care of His children and sends angels in person!*

By then, I was getting thirsty and bought a bottle of water for $3.50. Everything was expensive. I wasn't going to buy food! I sat down in the waiting area in a daze, and talked to a lady who was also flying to Sioux Falls. Everybody was very kind and helpful, and we had an uneventful flight. When we arrived, the same lady came and escorted me to the ground floor. I looked outside and saw my daughter and three beaming, happy grandchildren. Wow! I had made it!

I stayed in South Dakota for ten days, while my husband was overseas in Egypt, attending a mission conference. It was worth all the stress to spend ten days with my daughter's family, making special memories and sharing a room with my two granddaughters. I will always remember my first flight alone and the kindness of a helpful stranger – who must have been an angel in disguise. ❧

Fannie Troyer, 2010
Plains, MT

True or False – Angel Quiz

1. Angels were created by God. _____ (John 1:3; Neh. 9:6)
2. Angels are equal to God. _____ (1 Pt. 3:22)
3. All angels live in heaven. _____ (Jude 6; Mt. 25:41)
4. Angels are subject to death. _____ (Lu. 12:35; Lu. 20:36)
5. Angels worship God. _____ (Heb. 1:6; Rev. 7:11)
6. Angels and people are equal. _____ (Ps. 8:5; Heb. 2:7)
7. Some angels are married. _____ (Mk. 12:25; Lu. 20:35)
8. The born-again Christian knows some things angels cannot know. _____ (1Pet. 1:9-12)
9. Angels know when Christ will return. _____ (Mk. 13:32)
10. Angels will have part when Christ returns. _____ (Mt. 25:31; Mt. 13:39)
11. Angels pay special attention to children. _____ (Mt. 25:41)
12. The Bible says angels wear black. _____ (John 20:12; Mt. 28:2)

- Vera Overholt   ANSWERS:

1. True 2. False 3. False 4. False 5. True 6. False 7. False 8. True 9. False 10. True 11. True 12. False

23

Stranded!

"For He shall give His angels charge over thee, to keep thee in all thy ways." Psalm 91:11

We were camping in Baja California, Mexico, in the summer of 1989, and needed to go into the town of Santa Rosalía for supplies. On the way there, to my dismay and fear, we ran out of gas.

"Stay with the car, and I will walk into town," my husband said to me. I was afraid of all sorts of things and I decided to climb up the nearby mountain a short distance and watch the car from there. It was incredibly hot and I had no water.

Feeling vulnerable and helpless, I started praying and suddenly I heard a car. It was a dune buggy, stopping to give my husband a ride. As I watched from a distance, I really hoped some of the things we had heard about Mexico were not true.

There was nothing I could do, but wait. I tried to find some shade as it was getting even hotter. I lay in a sand lagoon and dozed off, trying to preserve my energy and not get too thirsty. After a while, my thirst hit hard, and really started to bother me. I tried not to think about it.

Suddenly, a woman appeared in very old, dark clothes. *They have to be hot,* I thought.

She had a whole gallon of water and said to me, "Drink." So I drank a little bit. I noted that the water tasted slightly salty.

She said again, very urgently, "You must drink more... *more!*" So I did, and again she did not think it was enough, and urged me to drink again.

I thanked her and said, "Look, you need your water, so don't give it all to me." She just nodded, and then left without saying anything more.

As I sat there, I began to think, "I don't see any houses." So I got up to look. As far as the eye could see, there were none. And then I noted that there were no footsteps or any other traces of someone walking. I wanted to see which way the old woman walked in case I needed more help, but I couldn't see anything. Where had she disappeared to so quickly?

After this, it wasn't long before I heard the dune buggy again, and the same people brought my husband back with some gas. That is when I remembered the scripture, Psalm 91:11, *"For He shall give His angels charge over thee, to keep thee in all thy ways."*

With thankful hearts, we made it to the gas station and finished our trip, but I will never forget how God provided water for me on that hot day in Mexico. He knew it needed to be a woman helping me, or I would have been terrified. I know God sent her, and I believe it was an angel. ❧

Veronika Snodgrass, 2015
Sarasota, FL

24

The Unexpected Answer to Prayer

"And he said unto me, 'The Lord, before whom I walk, will send His angel with thee, and prosper thy way...'" Genesis 24:40

O ne afternoon, around five years ago, I had some free time before my husband and children would be home from an evening event. I felt prompted to call Uncle Ted, my husband's elderly uncle, and invite him to go out with me for dinner.

We lived in Michigan at the time and Uncle Ted lived just across the Canadian border in Windsor, Ontario. My plan was to leave early enough so that I could comfortably have time to enjoy dinner with him, and then cross back over the border before nightfall. However, the evening progressed with wonderful conversation and before I knew it, it was dark.

I rarely went across the border on my own – normally my husband was with me – and I was a little afraid. In the darkness, I must have missed a sign, and got into the wrong lane. Before I knew it, I was surrounded by semi-trucks, instead of cars. With tall semi-trailers all around, I reached for my cell phone but realized it had run out of battery. With no way to contact anyone, the reality of my error in judgment to be crossing so late hit me full force. I felt very alone and afraid.

When I reached the border checkpoint and handed the guard my passport, I knew I would be lost since I was in the truck lane which exited to downtown Detroit, and I didn't know my way. The guard gave me detailed directions, but cautioned me about the area I was entering. "Lock your doors and do not get out of your car until you are safely in the suburbs."

I tried to look brave, swallowed hard and thanked the guard for his help. I knew he was right, because our congregation was involved in ministry outreach to inner-city Detroit, and I was aware of those areas which were not safe.

I attempted to follow his directions, but in the dark it was difficult and I soon realized I was lost. It was clear that I was in a rough area of downtown Detroit. *"Lord, please help me find my way,"* I finally prayed. *Why had I waited so long to pray?* As I prayed, a McDonalds came into sight. As I passed by, I noticed a very well-dressed elderly couple sitting at the window. They were looking at me. They were clearly out of place in this neighborhood, and I felt drawn to stop and ask them directions. I especially noticed the woman's face – she looked calm and serene, like someone I could trust.

I said one more prayer, mustered my courage, and pulled in and parked my car in the parking lot opposite the window where they were sitting. I raced inside and asked the elderly couple for directions. They were so sweet and caring, and kindly drew a map to help me get to where I needed to go. My hands were shaking and the elderly woman put her hand on my hand, as if to say, *"It's going to be okay."* I thanked them profusely and then dashed to my car again.

As I backed out of my parking spot, I fully intended to wave at them as I left. But as I turned to wave, to my astonishment, they were gone! *What? Impossible!* I could see all the way through the McDonalds from where I was parked and they were nowhere in sight. There simply wasn't time for this couple to have retreated out of sight in the time it took me to dash to my car.

Where did they go? And then it hit me. Could it be that in His great love, the Lord had sent His angels to rescue me? Yes! I believe he did! To this day, my eyes well up with tears as I picture the face of the sweet woman whom the Lord placed in my path to help me. I will never forget that night, lost in downtown Detroit, and the unexpected answer to my prayer. ✎

Kristine Krieger, 2016
Sarasota, FL

Other Names for Angels

References to angels are mentioned 283 times in the King James Version of the Bible. However, other names are also mentioned which refer to angels. Look up the references and fill in the blanks.

1. C_____ of G_____ (Ps. 68:17)
2. M_____ S_____ (Job 38:7)
3. C_____ of F_____ (2 Ki. 6:15-17)
4. H_____ H_____ (Lu. 2:13)
5. H_____ O_____ (Dan. 4:17)
6. W_____ (Dan. 4:17)
7. M_____ of G_____ (Judg. 13:6)
8. A_____ of H_____ (Dan. 4:35)
9. G_____ H_____ (Gen. 32:2)
10. T_____ R_____ (Mt. 13:39)

- Vera Overholt

25

The Unusual Mechanic

"...And, behold, angels came and ministered unto him." Matthew 4:11

I was around 21 years old at the time, and was encountering numerous challenges in my life. In hopes of obtaining spiritual victories in particular areas of struggle, I had been fasting for some time.

During this time, I needed to replace the front fender on my Volkswagen car. So I went to a pull-it-yourself junkyard to find the necessary part. After a while, I located a fender and began to take it off of the donor-parts car.

I removed all of the bolts and began prying with a crowbar. I pried with all my might but I could not get the fender loose. I was feeling very weak since I had not eaten in several days, and the hot, humid temperature added to my stress. At my wits' end, I prayed and cried out to God for help.

All at once, a gentleman walked up to me wearing a mechanic's uniform. He saw my predicament and told me to take the crowbar and pry it from a different angle. He showed me exactly where to pry. *Surely, that will not work*, I thought. It was too simple! But how could he know that I had been trying for half an hour with no success?

So, I did what the stranger suggested. I had nothing to lose. To my great amazement, it worked! The fender came right off!

I turned to thank him but he had already left. *How could he get away so soon?* I really wanted to thank my helper! I looked down the long aisles between the junk vehicles, but he was nowhere in sight.

I ran down one aisle and up the next, but found no one. Had the mechanic disappeared into another car to secure a part for himself? Or was this an angel sent from the Lord as a direct result of my prayer for assistance? *Thank, you, Lord!* ⊱

Matthias Overholt, 2004
Sarasota, FL

26

How God Got My Attention

"And Jacob went on his way, and the angels of God met him." Gen. 32:1

A round eight years ago, I was driving from my home near Sturgis, Michigan, on my way to our local Christian day school. Once a week, I would get together with a few other ladies to quilt for the annual school auction.

Suddenly, I saw a flashing blue light behind me, so I turned off the road to let the policeman pass me. But to my dismay, he pulled off right behind me. *Strange,* I thought, *I'm not speeding. Why would he be stopping me?* And then I thought of my seat belt. I had gotten into the habit of waiting until I was on the road to fasten it, and had forgotten to put it on when I left the house. Apparently, he had been following me for some time and had noticed a ways back that I didn't have it on, even though by the time he stopped me, I had it on.

As he stood at my driver's window, I explained to the officer how my 16-year-old daughter had been in an accident and we were told that if she had been wearing a seat belt, she would have died – and how that, ever since then, we were scared to wear it. He reminded me that he could tell me a hundred stories how seat belts had *saved* lives. I groaned inside as he handed me a $50.00 ticket. I decided I would have to wear it, whether I liked it or not.

A couple of weeks later, I was visiting at my son's house and left for home around 9:30 p.m. I was driving about half a mile down the road when I remembered. *Oh, I forgot the seat belt again,* I grumbled to myself.

I was approaching a stop sign, and thought I'd wait to put it on when I stopped. Suddenly, in my headlights, a large, white form appeared, right in front of me on the road! I braked, thinking I would hit it, and then suddenly it was gone. In a flash it came to me – *that was my angel!* It was beautiful, and I saw its wings spread out. But as quickly as I realized it was an angel, it was gone.

Immediately, I heard a kind voice in my ear, saying, *"Your seat belt is for your protection."* I knew it was the Lord speaking to me and I asked Him to forgive me for grumbling. I promised Him that from that moment, I would wear it and not complain anymore.

I believe that everyone that loves the Lord has a guardian angel (Ps. 91:11) and God needed to get my attention. Not only was He keeping me from potential harm but also helping me to be a good example to unbelievers watching my life. I got the message! And to this day, I always wear my seat belt. ❧

Mary Keely, 2013
Sturgis, MI

27

Marvin's Visitation

"Alas, O Lord God...because I have seen an angel of the Lord face to face." Judges 6:22

In my Christian Day School years, I was Marvin's best friend. His family, living at the foot of the mountain, was one of the poorer families. He seemed sensitive to spiritual matters and the supernatural.

Neither he nor I was part of the popular ones in our school or grade. Perhaps there were reasons we were not part of the inner group of students in grades seven through twelve. We both were quiet, and less aggressive or daring than some of the others, who talked of their audacious and forbidden experiences when they turned 16 and 17.

On the other hand, Marvin and I both enjoyed nature and activities that were stimulated by our high school course in Biology. He took a correspondence course in taxidermy, and was soon mounting large bugs, butterflies, and small animals. I don't recall any of our other classmates through the years talking about special interests in nature, or of hikes on the mountainside on a Sunday afternoon, such as Marvin and I enjoyed.

One night, Marvin awoke to a very unusual sight and experience. An angel appeared in his bedroom and came to the foot of his bed. The angel was holding a map of the world. Though not a word was spoken, the angel seemed to give a definite message as he pointed to a portion of the map. As the angel stood there pointing, Marvin felt that he was to be a missionary to some part of the world.

As this visitation happened over sixty years ago, I do not remember to what part of the map the angel was pointing, nonetheless, the message was clear to Marvin. He felt it was a call to missions.

A few years after graduation, Marvin married a school teacher who was teaching in our school. I was asked to be best man at the wedding.

But, later, Marvin developed an illness that brought him to a premature death. It seemed to be an untimely end of life of one who had the unusual visitation of an angel, and left me pondering many questions. Did Marvin misinterpret the message he seemed to have from the angel? Or, was the visit from the angel a gift, and meant to be an encouragement to one who was not accepted by the popular youth of his day?

It has been my observation that visits from angels are seldom made to the wealthy, elite or popular, but are made to the weak, the helpless or those living in poverty. It is obvious to me that the Lord often sends angels where there is a need, an emergency, or danger or to give a special message.

I will leave you to ponder this angel visitation of my friend, Marvin. Personally, I want to ask him my questions after we enter the pearly gates of glory. ☙

Urie Sharp, 2015
Bolivar, OH

28

Angels in the Room

"Are they not all ministering spirits, sent forth to minister for them who shall be heirs of salvation?" Hebrews 1:14

For a year, I had been fighting fatigue. My family doctor had warned me to make an appointment with a cardiologist. But I kept postponing it as I couldn't see my way through. When I wasn't working my part time job, I was caring for my husband, Sam, who was in the middle stages of Alzheimer's and in need of continual care and supervision.

One Tuesday morning, in April, 2012, I woke up with a confused mind. I was trying to do bookwork that day and things were not making sense. I started crying.

Soon after that, I had difficulty breathing. I remembered to take cayenne tincture and called my sister, who lived out of state. She, in turn, called her daughter and also a friend, who lived close by. I also called my son, who was just getting off of work. Before long, all three arrived.

My niece took me to Doctor's Hospital emergency room while my son stayed with my husband. By that time, my breathing had become easier, and I walked into the ER while my niece parked her car. The waiting room was empty, but soon an admittance worker appeared at the door and asked me what my problem was.

When I told him I had breathing problems and heaviness in my chest, I was rushed to a room and had an EKG performed.

After reviewing the test results, the male nurse said hastily, "You're having a heart attack, and you're not going home!"

The following day, more tests were taken. I was informed that I needed a new aortic valve and would be transported by ambulance to another hospital, where the surgery would be performed. On Thursday, I was moved to Sarasota Memorial Hospital and my oldest son flew down from Missouri to take over the care of his dad.

More tests were taken on Friday. By then, we were into the weekend, so the surgery was scheduled for early Monday morning. I felt at peace, as I had been anointed with oil by our senior pastor on Wednesday afternoon. I felt surrendered – ready to go, ready to stay.

On Sunday, I had a visitor from our congregation. I told her about the group that had come into my room to explain what would take place during my heart operation and how large the medical team would be.

"After they were finished speaking," I relayed to my friend, "I reminded them that God would also be in the room. I wish I would have told them, 'The angels will also be in the room.'"

After my visitor left, a thought came to me. *I think I once heard a song about "angels in the room."* That evening, when my son came in with his laptop computer, I asked him if he could look up that song. He found it, and it was so beautiful and comforting to me.

On Monday, two more sons and a daughter-in-law had arrived from Ohio, in time to see me go into surgery at 6:30 a.m. I didn't wake up until Tuesday morning at 2:30, and then, for only a short period. A number of hours later, at 6:30 a.m., they moved me to a private room and that woke me. After the nurses left the room, my first thought was, *there are angels in the room!* That thought kept ringing in my mind, like a blanket covering my pain.

That afternoon, a good friend stopped in and brought me a balloon. To my amazement, there were pictures of six angels, with the words, *"For He shall give His angels charge over thee to keep thee in all thy ways."*

Remarkably, the balloon stayed inflated for around five months, the hardest period of my recovery. And it reminded me constantly that there were angels in the room. ❧

Martha Hostetler, 2015
Sarasota, FL

❧ Compiler's Note: At the time of this first edition, in 2016, Martha is again going through a very difficult time, following a debilitating stroke. In her own words, "I am longing to be in the presence of Jesus and His angels, and I want to encourage each one reading this story to live for Him so that we can meet on that beautiful shore."

The song that comforted Martha in the hospital:

Angels in the Room

She is close to death – but she is not afraid,
Angels waiting for the order, to carry her away;
They're gathered 'round her bedside, she's the only one who sees,
She will draw her final breath, and away with them she'll leave.

> *Angels in the room, she's run her final race, They've come*
> *To carry her to heaven, there to see her Savior's face;*
> *Angels in the room to take her to her great reward,*
> *No need for sadness or gloom, there are angels in the room.*

Angels in the room, when you run your final race,
They will carry you to heaven, there to see your Savior's face;
Angels in the room, to take you to your great reward,
No need for sadness or gloom, there'll be angels in the room.

- Chuck Day

29

God's Presence in Sorrow

"But ye are come unto Mount Zion, and unto the city of the living God, the heavenly Jerusalem, and to an innumerable company of angels..."
Hebrews 12:22

Dad's health was causing us great concern. On May 16, 2013, it was obvious that he was trying to participate in our family reunion, yet he wasn't feeling his best. He mentioned feeling dizzy and having stomach trouble.

At a visit to a doctor in Grayling, Michigan, medication was prescribed, but Dad continued getting worse and started to become confused. On June 10, he was taken to Midland Emergency Room, around 70 miles away. The doctor there advised that he see a psychiatrist as soon as possible.

The days following the emergency room visit, I checked in on Dad, and saw him getting more discouraged and confused. He would cry as he asked, "What is wrong?" Soon after that, he was having trouble talking clearly or walking steadily.

One day, while having difficulty making a sandwich, he began to cry uncontrollably. That afternoon it was decided that he would need to go to Midland hospital, as Dad in his confusion talked of seeing things that were not there. It was hard to see him in that condition. But leaving him at Midland hospital was harder. I kept in contact with the hospital staff all week.

Family and friends began to arrive for support. A spinal tap and an EKG were performed and sent out for further testing. The attitude of the physician left our family dissatisfied, and we began to discuss a transfer to another hospital. At the advice of our Uncle Ernest, we agreed that each of us would pray about what to do, then meet again the next day.

Our meeting the next day concluded with the decision that we three brothers would take Dad to the Mayo Clinic in Rochester, Minnesota. But that meant a twelve-hour drive or a three-hour flight, and it was urgent that we get him there as soon as possible. We needed to find a way to transfer him and make the necessary arrangements. Providentially, I met an employee at work who was not supposed to be working, but who had felt prompted to come in that morning. Through him, we found a charter flight to Mayo.

Prior to leaving, my brother Richard arranged a taxi to take us from the Rochester airport to the clinic. He called a phone number obtained from a list of taxi services found on the Internet. The man who answered the phone spoke in broken English and said he would provide the thirty-minute taxi ride for only thirty dollars.

It was a nice summer day and we had clear skies for flying. It was special for us three brothers to be flying with our dad, something I had never expected to do. The pilot gave us an arrival time and Richard tried calling the taxi driver. We had forgotten that we would gain an hour and had started earlier than planned.

Cell phone service was not good at 8,000 feet and Richard couldn't get through until we started to descend, about fifteen minutes before we were to land. He told the taxi driver that we were early and had not been able to make contact with him sooner. Then he lost the connection. Five minutes before landing, Richard reached him again and said we were ready to land. The driver said he would be there.

We landed at the large, international airport as a private, business flight, so there was no security or anything to delay us. We helped Dad into the wheelchair and into the terminal as soon as we could, as it was hot on the asphalt. Richard was coming in with the last of the luggage when his phone rang.

It was the taxi driver, and he was waiting for us. He was a tall, friendly, Hispanic man. When we arrived at the hospital, he drove us to the walk-in emergency room entrance, but then backed out and said, "I know better." He took us to the ambulance emergency room entrance instead. We paid the helpful driver and he left. The admittance went quickly since we had avoided the waiting room and the paperwork had been sent ahead from Midland.

I had gone back to look for a motel when the team of doctors brought the diagnosis, at around 11:00 a.m. Dad had an incurable illness, they could do nothing for him, and we might as well return home! I came back to the hospital just after the doctors had left. We called the family and then had to share the diagnosis with Dad. How much would he understand?

We walked into the room and stood around Dad's bed. He looked at us as if he had been waiting and he tried to ask what the doctors had found. We told him everything they had told us. We all cried with Dad and with one another. We talked and prayed with Dad quite a while. His mind cleared for a short time and he understood what we said. His crying after that point was completely different – more a resigned cry than a confused one.

I called Keith, the pilot, to schedule the return flight. The hospital staff was very helpful to arrange things for us. They called the taxi company to take us to the airport, but did not get an answer. They left a message but did not hear back, so they called the number again and a woman answered. In an agitated voice, she said she didn't do any taxi work and we were calling her personal cell phone number. We checked and double checked the number they had dialed, and it was the same number Richard had used while on the plane.

The staff then called a different number, and a new taxi driver came to take us to the airport. We showed them our telephone list with the company name and number. We then described the man – and he said they did not have any Hispanic people working for them, or anyone else who did not speak fluent English. Who was this driver who had picked us up 24 hours earlier?

Keith was waiting at the airport with a different airplane. The wind was stronger and picking up, and the weather monitor revealed that a big storm was coming. We were leaving just ahead of it. In spite of that, the takeoff was very smooth again, and we headed home to Mio, Michigan.

We tried to enjoy the scenery. Dad was taking the trip home very well. As we got closer to the Mio airport, reality hit me. I never thought that someday we would be flying into this airport with Dad, with the realization that he was dying.

As we circled over the community and arrived at the airport, we were amazed to see all the family, friends and neighbors who were there to welcome us home. During the past 40 hours we had very little sleep or food, but I never felt tired or hungry in that time. God was providing the strength! We took Dad home and settled him in for the night.

The next ten days were special to me. It was like one, long reunion. We spent a lot of time around Dad's bedside, talking to him, singing and praying. We took turns staying with him at night. We were coming together daily, and Dad seemed to be the same, day after day. But when we looked back a few days, we could see that he was steadily getting weaker.

Uncle Ernest and Aunt Mary slept in the basement and traded off with the ones that stayed for the night. We really appreciated their help and support. The church families brought in two meals a day for everyone. Every evening we planned how to get everyone together if something changed.

By Sunday, June 21, we could see that Dad wouldn't live much longer. He was not responding much anymore when we talked to him, and he gradually grew weaker. We were all together when he peacefully breathed his last. So many friends and family came for Dad's funeral. I thought of all those people whom Dad had known, that he would have wanted to visit with.

In spite of the pain we were going though, God was so close to us. Through all of this, I don't know how we would have been able to take it without Him.

As I think back, I still wonder about that taxi driver, whose helpful assistance eased Dad's discomfort upon arrival at the Mayo Clinic. He must have been an angel. I have never had an experience like that before or since. How special, that God intervened in this way beyond our human reasoning, and was looking out for even the smallest details of our lives during this time of sorrow and transition. ✍

Elmer Miller, 2014
Sears, MI

30

My Father Sees an Angel

"For the Son of man shall come in the glory of His Father with His angels; and then He shall reward every man according to his works."

Matthew 16:27

My father, too, was privileged to see an angel. But before I tell you about that, I want to share a few things that I am thankful for about "Pop" – the name we always called him. Pop wasn't a perfect father, and had shortcomings that he struggled with. But I want to mention a few of his good points that I appreciate, even more since I am older.

I grew up in the middle of eleven children, feeling secure in our sheltered home environment. My parents, John and Alta Sommers, were not wealthy, and we worked hard as a family of thirteen to make ends meet. We lived on a farm near North Canton, Ohio, and later, we moved near Hartville. Pop farmed for a living and milked cows. Both Pop and Mom rose before dawn, working long hours each day. He also bought the weekly groceries since Mom never learned to drive. We children helped to grow and preserve our own food – from the garden, the orchard, and the animals that we raised. When I was around eight years old, in 1939, World War II broke out. We worked hard during those years, and lived, ate and dressed simply, but that was our general way of life. My parents were frugal and saving, and nothing was wasted.

Although my father was never a church leader, he saw to it that we all faithfully attended church services on Sundays, or whenever any special meetings were held through the week. We were members at the Maple Grove Conservative Mennonite Church. (The years of my involvement in that congregation, 1939–1959, were good years, filled with times of fellowship with friends, lots of singing, youth gatherings, old-time revival preachers, missionary speakers, summer Bible schools, and singing schools. Those years were a stabilizing influence in my Christian growth.) My father was a peace-maker. When there was a conflict or disagreement in the church, he voiced his concern that we all work together.

My father and mother were both very hospitable and unselfish in opening their doors to guests. My older siblings often invited young people who were visiting our congregation or were participating in choral singing groups. There were also young people from Grantsville, Maryland, who often came to Hartville on weekends, and many of them found their way to our house, which became known as "the hotel on the hill" (by that time, we lived on top of the hill on Midway Street). I remember how one family often visited us, inevitably dropping in unannounced around meal time. We also had guests from various parts of the world, including Germany, India, Korea and Scotland. One distinguished German guest was the interpreter for Billy Graham, when his crusades were held in Germany.

Another gathering at our house was informal music-practice, held in our big kitchen on the hill. Up and down the scale we went, learning to sing the notes correctly. My parents also entertained homeless people – called "tramps" in those days – who walked the streets, looking for hand-outs. (See my sister Ruby's story on page 71, *The Tramp*). I remember, too, my parents' kindness, when I worked with children in a mission Sunday school in Canton, Ohio. I would often invite them to our home in the country. To my regret, it seemed I often took my parents' hospitality for granted.

I have fond memories of our devotional time as a family each evening. Before going to bed, we sang and had prayer, which was important to Pop and Mom. We sang from *New Spiritual Songs,* a Brethren-in-Christ songbook (Eli and Lydia Hostetler, my aunt and uncle, were Brethren-in-Christ). When I began traveling and singing with Joseph Overholt and his twin brother, John – the man whom I would later marry – my parents supported me in those ventures. When I began teaching school, I always had a place to come home to, and I didn't marry until I was 33. These are some of the memories that come to mind as I think about my father, and some of the blessings I took for granted.

But now, back to when Pop saw an angel. His health began failing from heart-related problems when he was in his early eighties. But he did not want to go to the hospital. As time went on, he was getting very low and was in bed most of the time. When I prayed with him, he also prayed. He always started his prayers with *"Our kind, heavenly, Father, we do thank You…."*

One morning, when my mother went into his room to check on him, Pop said he had seen an angel standing by his bed! This was very comforting to both of my parents, a reassurance of God's love and presence with them in the final days of Pop's life. ◈

Vera Overholt, 2016
Sarasota, FL

❧ Compiler's Note: Soon after this encounter with the angel, we finally needed to take Pop to the hospital, where he died on April 13, 1982, at age 85. He was the only grandfather our children knew, and they have many good memories of interacting with him in his elderly years, when they knew him.

31

Never Alone - Hallelujah!

"I will never leave thee, nor forsake thee." Hebrews 13:5. "He that overcometh, the same shall be clothed in white raiment; and I will not blot out his name out of the book of life, but I will confess his name before My Father, and before His angels." Revelation 3:5

One of the evangelistic programs of Life Ministries is gospel literature distribution in third world countries, with thousands of dollars' worth of literature being distributed every year. But it all began with Haiti, when my husband, Lester, had a vision to share God's love through literature in that desperately needy country. After many years of storing the literature in temporary locations in Haiti, we needed a permanent distribution center. So Lester contacted the Blue Ridge Mission and together they came up with a plan.

In February, 2000, Lester and I, along with another married couple, John and Dorcas Bomberger, went to Haiti to begin building the guest house and distribution center on the Blue Ridge Mission compound near Port-au-Prince. Blue Ridge had told us that if we would build the guest house, they would give us the land to build it on and they would take it over after ten years. The guest house apartments would be upstairs and the bottom floor would be used to store the literature. Large garage doors would be installed on either side so that trucks could drive through to pick up literature for churches and schools.

Now, here we were in Haiti to begin this building project, excited to see the distribution center becoming a reality. But it was extremely warm, and by the end of the second week, I was becoming very concerned about Lester's health.

"Are you drinking enough water," I frequently asked him. I knew that when he got really hot, he could get very sick. We didn't know what his condition was at that time, but he would have flu-like symptoms with high fever and dehydration.

On the last night of our two-week stay in Haiti, we were invited to eat supper with our friends, Lamar and Miriam Nolt. They were the administrators of the Christian Aid Ministries compound, and we had been staying in their guesthouse. But after working all day in the hot sun, Lester came home and lay across the bed. I didn't hear the words that I loved hearing from him, *"I love you, Honey."* Instead, I heard the three words I most dreaded, "I'm sick, Honey." He became extremely ill and his temperature climbed to 105°. He couldn't take anything in, though he hadn't eaten since lunch.

We prayed fervently for wisdom to know what to do. With Lester ill, and being far from my family, I reached out for counsel from Lamar, who was the age of my oldest son. "Do you know where we can find an American doctor? *Anywhere?*"

"No, I don't!" he responded.

We stayed up all night, and John, who was traveling with us, helped me drip water into Lester's mouth. If we gave him even a teaspoon, he would dry heave and bring it up. Another couple, who were staying at the CAM guesthouse that night, joined us for prayer in the living room, crying out to God for help and wisdom.

I continued praying as I cared for him throughout the night, dripping water into his mouth and wiping his head and body with cool water to bring his fever down. It dropped to 103°, still dangerously high. What were we to do? There was no hospital in the area at that time, and we were way out in the country.

At 5:30 the next morning, Lamar came up from his house to check on us. "You were up all night, weren't you? I saw the lights on! Why don't we head out into the country? I heard there is an American doctor in the clinic around two hours from here."

Well, if you have ever been in Haiti, you know the roads are terribly rough. But we had to do something! So I agreed, and Lamar helped us put Lester in the car and we headed out on the rough country roads. The whole way, I kept dripping water in his mouth and kept washing his face off with water to keep him cool. His fever was so high that he was almost delirious. I thought I had plenty of water along, but wished I had taken a lot more. In Haiti, you have to buy all your water. It barely lasted until we reached the clinic, almost two hours later. Lamar blew the horn, and they opened the gate and we rushed in.

"I will never go home, I will die out here," Lester rasped as we arrived. "I am so weak. I need a doctor immediately! I've got to get in!" We quickly helped him into the clinic but there was no place to sit. The whole place was full, though it was still early morning. All the chairs were being used, and people were even sitting on the floor. Dogs, cats and chickens mingled with the throng of people waiting to be helped, while dark-skinned nurses tried to maintain order.

They all stared at us as we entered. We were certainly an unusual sight in that remote area. They tried to speak with us and welcomed us, speaking Creole. I didn't speak their language, but Lamar did. "We want to see a doctor," Lamar told them.

"American doctor? No! No doctor. He went home two days ago!" My heart sank. Had we come all the way out here, almost two hours, on all those rough roads, and there was no doctor?

"I have to sit down," Lester said weakly. "I'm sure I'm going to die."

"Honey, we're not going to believe that," I responded urgently. I walked through the whole clinic and found an old, school desk. I pulled it over to where he was standing in the waiting room and helped him sit down. He laid his head on the desk.

"Water, water," he kept repeating. "Honey, I need water." But our water was gone. So, again I walked through the clinic, and in the next room was a five gallon bottle of water! But I had no cup. So I prayed, *"Lord, I found the water. I found the desk. Please give me a cup."*

Just then, a lady came in with five little cups to take to the water fountain. I pointed at her cups and asked her for one.

"Oui, oui" (WEE – *"yes"*), she said, and handed one to me.

"Oh, thank you! Praise the Lord!" I gratefully filled a cup and took it to Lester.

"I need a doctor," Lester groaned. I looked all around, but there was clearly no doctor anywhere in the clinic.

"What do we do now?" Lamar asked in concern.

"I'll never make it back if I don't get IVs," replied Lester. "I'm too weak. I won't make it to the airplane unless we find one." I knew it was the only thing that would help Lester in his dehydrated condition.

So, once more I walked through the clinic, leaving Lester with his head on the desk. I cried out to God for help. Suddenly, in front of me there were two men standing. They wore knee-length pants, with long stockings that came up to their knees, and boots, and looked like Dutch men from a century ago. Long, bushy hair framed their faces. I had never seen men dressed like that, other than in pictures.

"Ma'am, what do you want?" they asked kindly, in English.

"We need a doctor! There is no doctor here today. Is there any doctor in the village or anywhere close by? The nurses have no idea what to do. We need IVs!"

"We will get you a doctor," they responded. And then, all of a sudden, they were gone. And immediately, somebody walked in through the door, a Haitian doctor! I was astounded. *How could they have gotten a doctor so quickly? How could that have happened? These men who were helping us had to have been sent by God!*

"May I help you?" the doctor asked us, in Creole.

"We need IVs. Please, don't you have any IVs? Look in a cupboard," I pleaded.

"No! No IVs. But I will look." So he left and looked in the cupboard, and to our delight, there was an IV bag! Now, if he could just find a needle! We began praying, "Lord, please, we need a sterilized needle." Sure enough, the doctor found a needle.

"I can't take it here, lying on this desk," said Lester. "I have to find another place to lie down." So I went to the next room, and there was an old, office desk.

"Honey, would you be able to lie here on this desk?" He couldn't stretch out on it but was able to lie sideways, but he had no pillow. So I put my purse under his head, and the doctor put the IV into his arm. I stood there and held the bag because there was nothing to hook it on, until Lamar found an old, rusty coat rack to hold it up. Now we could only wait and pray. Even though there was only one IV bag available, it would take a couple of hours for it to drain.

Meanwhile, I wanted to thank the two foreign-looking men who had spoken with me. "Where are those men?" I asked the doctor. "I didn't see any men," he replied.

"But I saw them! I saw two men and they talked to me. I hadn't even finished talking to them, and they vanished, and you walked in!" I tried to explain what had happened, but it was obvious he didn't know about the two men. I soon found out that nobody saw them. The nurses were right there, and they had not seen them either. I never saw them again – they were gone.

I was in awe as I realized what God had done. I had just met two angels! We were not alone! Maybe Lester would still pull through! But I was feeling desperate to leave the clinic in order to catch our afternoon flight back to Miami.

"Honey, do you think you're strong enough to go out in the car?" I kept asking. We had to get him on that airplane, because he didn't think he would live.

"No, I can't. I'm not going to make it anyway, why don't you just let me die?" he would answer me in despair. And I kept saying, "No, we're not going to let you die!" Though he looked very ill, I was sure American Airlines would let him get on the plane to take him to the Miami hospital, because there was no local, Haitian hospital that could help him in his condition.

The IV was dripping so slowly. And he was still so weak. "Honey, I just need water." We kept putting water on him, and I was praying constantly, quietly, over Lester. *"Lord, please, if You want to take him home, please don't take him home here. I don't want him to die in Haiti. Lord, if You need to, please let him die in the United States, so we're home. Lord, please heal his body. You can touch him if that is Your will."*

The doctor kept coming in, saying, "That's all I have, I don't have anything else to give him – just this one." He seemed concerned and at a loss to know what else to do.

At 10:30 a.m., Lester finally said, "Honey, we have to go. It took us almost two hours to get here, and we have to get to the airport so we can leave at 2:00. I think I can make it now, if you hold the bag." We unhooked it from its rusty wire perch, and I held the bag up as Lamar helped him to walk out of the clinic. The doctor had come out to help him, too. He took an old wire to fasten the bag to the handle above the door. The doctor and Lamar did not want me to hold it the whole way back to the mission compound.

I was uneasy, knowing how critical it was to keep the bag dripping properly for Lester. But I complied, and focused on lowering Lester's fever by pouring water on his head, praying all the while that we would get to the airplane in time. We started out, happy that we were heading back and that Lester had an IV dripping into his body and that he felt strong enough to get in the car. We called ahead and asked John and Dorcas to be ready to leave instantly with our luggage.

We had only gone one mile down the road and we went over a bump and the bag came unhooked! The needle popped out of Lester's arm and we couldn't get it back in. So there went the IV. I thought, *"Lord, please. Why did this have to happen? I wanted to hold it so badly. Please show us where we can get another one! That one was supposed to get us all the way to the airplane so that it could drip during the flight and keep him going until we got to Miami!"* I was thinking fast. Where could we go? Lamar remembered there was a Haitian doctor close to the airport that might have one. *Lord, help us to get there in time!*

It was a fast and furious drive back to the mission compound on the bumpy roads, and Lester was miserable and suffering. "Oh, I'm in so much pain! My fever's so high! Honey, just let me die, I just want to go to heaven." All the while, I was praying. Finally, we got back. John had the suitcases ready, and we crowded into the vehicle and rushed to the airport. Lester lay on the reclined front seat and I kept working with him from behind. Lamar quickly stopped at the doctor's office and sure enough, they had an IV bag, and the life-saving fluid was hooked up once again. This time I held it until we reached the airport – I wasn't taking any chances.

When we arrived at the airport and had boarded our flight, Lester was placed on the first row with me right beside him. He put his head back on the seat and said resignedly, "I'm not going to make it back to Miami, Honey. The Lord's going to be with you. I'm not going to make it." And then he got quiet. He wouldn't talk the rest of the way. I kept rubbing his arm and praying and watching that he was breathing. John and Dorcas were praying, too, that we'd get back.

Relief washed over me as we landed in Miami, where an ambulance was waiting for him. "Come on, Mrs. Miller, we've got to get going! Get in the ambulance, we've got to run," the paramedics urged me.

I encouraged John and Dorcas to catch their connecting flight, but they refused and wanted to stay to help us. So John and I hurried down the hall to change our tickets while Dorcas stayed with Lester. We arrived at the office just as the ticket-counter agent was coming out the door and locking it.

"Sir, wait," I called. "You see that ambulance over there? That's my husband. We came from Haiti. And these are our tickets home. We were supposed to go on to Harrisburg, but we can't – he's going to the hospital. Can you please mark them, so we don't have to pay for new tickets?" He could have refused, but he unlocked the door and went back in and made the changes on the tickets so there would be no additional charge. "Thank you, Lord!" I exclaimed.

I ran to the waiting ambulance and wanted to climb in the back with Lester but they said I had to sit in the front. I sat down, and started crying. *Dear Lord, we got here, thank you Lord, we got here!*

"It's alright, ma'am," the driver consoled me, "It's alright." He seemed genuinely concerned about me.

"I'm not crying about my husband's condition, I'm crying for joy that we got here to Miami!" Of course, he had no idea about the ordeal that we had been through in the last 24 hours. "I know the Lord Jesus. God got us here, and that's why I'm praying." I couldn't stop crying and praising God that we got there. I looked over at him, and he said, "Now what did you say about God?" I had the opportunity to share the whole plan of salvation with him as we drove to the hospital, and also gave him some gospel tracts.

We were taken to a small hospital and when we arrived, there was no place for Lester in the emergency room. But they found a bed and put him in the hall. We weren't allowed to stay overnight since the place was filled to capacity and there was no room, and he was in the hall. But it was actually better that he was in the hall since they could constantly monitor him. Lester's IV bag was steadily dripping and dripping – a beautiful sight!

John, Dorcas and I found a motel to stay overnight, and we praised the Lord continually that we had made it, though I was emotionally exhausted. In the morning, we went back to the hospital.

Lester was in the hospital three days, but the doctors couldn't find what was wrong with him, and were puzzled by his persistently high fever. They finally got enough IV fluid into him to stabilize him for his flight back to Harrisburg. We were overjoyed to get home, and God's care for us during our crisis in Haiti lingered in our minds. We would never forget how God sent his angels to help us when we felt so alone, far from home. Our hearts were overflowing with the words of Psalm 34:1-4: *"I will bless the LORD at all times: His praise shall continually be in my mouth. My soul shall make her boast in the LORD: the humble shall hear thereof, and be glad. O magnify the LORD with me, and let us exalt His name together. I sought the LORD, and He heard me, and delivered me from all my fears."*

Part 2

T he years 2000 and 2001 were difficult years for us with Lester in and out of the hospital. It wasn't until November, 2001, that we found out what was causing his reoccurring high fevers, after all those years of not knowing what we had been dealing with. It was called *autoimmune vasculitis*, a rare condition from a virus in his veins, which may have been passed from his mother in the womb. The virus causes inflammation and swelling of the blood vessels, and as in Lester's case, bleeding.

When he was hospitalized at Thanksgiving, he felt he might not live very long and wanted the whole family to come to the hospital and take communion together. So we met in a private room, with Lester in his hospital gown, sharing the bread and wine that we had brought with us. A quiet sense of peace pervaded. Would it be our last time to celebrate Christ's suffering and love in this way? Lester was in the hospital over Thanksgiving, but two days later he got better and came home. He went back to work at Life Ministries and said he felt really good.

One day, in mid-December, he said, "After Christmas, we're going to plan a praise celebration for the church. I'm healed!" It was December 13. "I'm healed, I know I am. I'm going to pick songs and call a group to sing at our Sunday morning service." Among the 22 people he called to help sing was my mother, who was the choir alto at that time.

We looked at the calendar to pick a day. "Which Sunday do you want?" I asked him.

"I want the last Sunday of December," he replied. So we began planning the celebration service, and he was excited and started writing down his story.

But close to Christmas, he started bleeding again and was taken to Lancaster General Hospital. From there he needed to be transferred to Johns Hopkins Hospital in Maryland. God miraculously arranged a house close to the hospital that was large enough for our entire family to stay there together. But the bleeding wouldn't stop, in spite of all the blood Lester was continuously receiving. After 72 units of blood had been given in five days, the doctors asked him, "How long do you want this to go on?"

"I don't," he replied. "Let's take everything off, and we'll pray. And if God keeps me going, then I know I'm healed and I'll be alright – He can stop the bleeding. But if not, then God will take me home." So everything was taken off, including the oxygen. He still had a good heart but he was steadily growing weaker.

Around 5:00 p.m., on Christmas Day, we were sitting around his bed, when he suddenly looked up and exclaimed, "Honey! Look how bright it is up there!" We had started dimming the lights and it was actually dark in the room. "It's so bright! Oh, it's gorgeous! It's brighter than anything I ever saw."

"Honey, what do you see?" I asked.

"Look up! Don't you see that?"

"No. You're here in bed, but you must be seeing heaven," I replied.

"Oh, don't you see the green grass, and all the trees? They are so beautiful and loaded with fruit. And there are soldiers up there at the gate. And it's so bright. Look at those beautiful gardens! I see eagles. And I hear bells ringing! Look at all the people! Oh, there's a little girl running in the green grass and she looks so healthy! Everyone looks like they do down here, but they look so healthy – no one looks sick. There's Peter – I can't wait to ask him some things when I get there! I hear singing!" Suddenly Lester began singing "Marvelous Grace" and our family joined in singing. He also sang, "Saved by the Blood of the Crucified One" and "Redeemed by the Blood of the Lamb," and we would all sing together.

During his last eighteen hours, Lester talked about heaven off and on, describing in detail what he was seeing. He talked about how there are angels everywhere and how everything is so bright and so beautiful and so great. He talked continuously about how gorgeous it is. He quoted Psalm 23 three different times and we would join in reciting those comforting verses. He would speak a few words, and then lie quietly, and then he would speak some more about what he was seeing or he would quote verses, such as, *"God is my refuge and strength."*

At one point, he exclaimed, "Jesus said, *'I go to prepare a place for you,'* and, Honey, you should see the mansions! They are way beyond anything we ever saw. Everyone has a different mansion. Honey, wherever you go, tell everyone not to miss heaven, it's more beautiful than I can ever describe! And the gate is so wide and friends and relatives are saying, *'Come on, Lester! Come on!'* The next couple of days will be amazing! God is going to do a miracle."

Then he looked at us and spoke words of blessing over each one of us. When he looked at me, he said, "Honey, you're a rose and a lily. So many times, you could have left me. Why did you stay with me? Through all those operations – I was so sick every time and I had such high fevers. Would you marry me if I would ask you to do it all over again?"

"Yes, I would," I answered. "Think of all the Lord has brought us through and how He was with us through those seven operations. And after every one, He gave you a vision of a new ministry to start – from starting *East District Mennonite Church* to *Maranatha Christian School,* to Haitian evangelism trips with young people, to *Sharon Mennonite Bible Institute,* to *Berean Bible Conference,* to *Life Ministries* to *Life Fellowship.* Every time, we prayed and you took it on. Of course, I'd do it all over again. Yes, it was a long journey but we had happiness in it. And when those dreams and visions were fulfilled, we were always so blessed."

Around 11:00 the next morning, Lester said to me, "I don't think it's going to be long. Jesus is coming – I'm going to give you a big hug." And again he hugged me. "I love you, Honey. How are you going to do it without me here on earth?"

"Honey, with the help of a wonderful family – I'm going to be alright, and God is going to take care of me."

He said, "Oh, I wish I had a lot more money to give you, how are you ever going to make it?

"Don't worry about that, that's the least thing."

Then he released me and said, "I want you to get married again, if you can."

"Let's not talk about that right now, Honey. I'm married to *you*. I love you."

But he continued, "I think I know who's going to ask you," and I replied, "I don't want to know." He was being unselfish right to the end, putting my needs first.

After resting awhile, he exclaimed, "Oh, there you are, *Honsey Babe*, I was looking all over for you! I want us to go to heaven together!"

"I'm here rubbing your feet," I replied. "You always loved that."

"Well, come and be right beside me. I don't want to go without you. In a couple of minutes, I'll feel good! I have such peace." Then he hugged me so tight that I could hardly breathe.

"Honey," I replied, when I could get my breath, "we probably can't go together. But I will come later!"

"Dad, don't hold her so tight," our sons, Wendell and Keith, urged him.

"But I want her to go along and I want her to be in heaven with me," Lester insisted.

Our children were standing around the room, and seven doctors and nurses were standing there with us. They watched us in wonder, and asked how we could be calmly singing instead of screaming and being upset about Lester dying. "It's because we know he loves Jesus and is ready to go to heaven," I responded. Right then, we had the privilege of sharing the gospel with them.

Suddenly, I felt my chest tightening and had difficulty breathing. "Oh, I feel like I'm having a heart attack," I gasped.

"Honey!" Lester looked at me with concern in his eyes.

One of the nurses looked at me and insisted, "Come with us!"

"No, I want to stay here with him and see the angels come for him."

"Well," they said, "he's not going now. He could live three days yet. Look at his heart – it's good. And we're not going to let you die with all those wonderful children and grandchildren that need you. We want to check your heart to make sure you're not having a heart attack. Come with us!"

Lester hugged me and then raised his hands in a sweeping motion, as if to say, *"You need to go on."* His care for me was so apparent, in spite of being so weak.

"Just come with me, he'll be all right," a nurse said. I went reluctantly, because I wanted to stay there with Lester. My girls, Crystal and Starla, said they were going with me. "You'd better not, if you want to be with your Daddy when the angels come for him," I told them.

But the girls still wanted to go with me and had cell phones, and my sons had theirs. We agreed that the boys would call if they saw the end was near. So we went down the hall into a private room, and I waited for the doctor to come and examine me. Just then, I heard my son, Wendell, asking a nurse, "Which curtain is Mother behind?"

I pulled aside the curtain and said, "He's gone, isn't he?"

"Yes," answered Wendell quietly. "He's gone. He never said another word. He took a big breath, and he was gone." They didn't even have time to call us! *"Oh, Lord, why? I wanted to be with him!"* I was with him the last year and ten months during his acute periods of illness and I wanted to be with him to the end of his life on earth.

My youngest son, Keith, put his arm around me. "Mother, every night you said, 'God is the blessed controller of all things.' Now I'm saying back to you, 'God is the blessed controller of all things.' If you can't accept that, we're going for counseling!" It was just what I needed.

"Alright, I'm not going to ask 'Why,'" I told him, and all of us went back to Lester's room. We walked in, and I went to his bed and wrapped him in my arms, and began singing his favorite song, *"Face to face with Christ, my Savior, face to face what will it be, when with rapture I behold Him, Jesus Christ, who died for me."* The whole family stood around the bed, grieving and crying together, looking at our beloved husband and father and grandfather who was no longer with us.

God took him home the day after Christmas, 2001. His memorial service was held on the exact Sunday he was planning to celebrate his healing. But God had other plans, and gave him perfect healing. He was having the celebration he had planned! Our celebration down here was laced with the sorrow of parting. But his celebration at the gate of heaven held only joy – a grand reunion with relatives and friends, with angels all around.

At his graveside, a dove flew directly over the canopy where we were gathered. It was unusual to see a dove in such cold weather, with five inches of snow on the ground, and it reminded us of the presence of God's Spirit and His peace in the midst of our pain. The words of the poem, *Finally Home*, which Lester liked so well, had become a reality:

But just think…

> *Of stepping on shore – And finding it Heaven!*
> *Of touching a hand – And finding it God's!*
> *Of breathing new air – And finding it celestial!*
> *Of waking up in glory – And finding it home!*
> *- L. E. Singer (Poem used on Lester's memorial card)*

"Praise be to the God and Father of our Lord Jesus Christ, who has blessed us in the heavenly realms with every spiritual blessing in Christ." Ephesians 1:3 (NIV). ❧

Betty Miller, 2016
Landisville, PA

❧ Compiler's Note: In 2014, after being a widow for over twelve years, Betty married again, and in her own words, "I had the incredible joy of marrying another, precious *Lester Miller*. Praise the Lord! Only He could do something like this!" Together, they have seven married children, one unmarried son, 25 grandchildren and eight great-grandchildren. They live half the year in Lancaster County, Pennsylvania, and half the year in Sarasota, Florida, remaining active in prison ministry, teaching *Bondage to Freedom* and *Conflict Resolution* seminars.

32

Starburst

"For I am persuaded, that neither death, nor life, nor angels, nor principalities, nor powers, nor things present, nor things to come... shall be able to separate us from the love of God..." Romans 8:38

"I'm sorry, Jacinda," Mom said tearfully, "but the doctor said we have to move close to the hospital in Cincinnati while you're in treatment." I didn't think my stomach could hurt any worse than it already did from being sick, but Mom's words were like a kick in the gut. Ohio was 400 miles away!

I was only fifteen at the time, and my illness prevented me from participating in a lot of things that other girls my age enjoyed. At least I had my horse. Nothing could separate me from my beloved horse. At least that's what I thought, until Mom said we had to move.

Starburst, a beautiful, red, quarter horse, was a gift from Mom. She bought her for me after watching us virtually flying together across the ranch we had visited, while looking for the perfect horse. What mom didn't know at the time was that no one had ever ridden Starburst before I did. She was what you'd call a *green* horse – when a horse is in the first, early phases of being trained, but nowhere near being ready to ride – until I showed up, that is.

Starburst *asked* me to ride her. She really did. I was standing on the rail of the corral gate watching her circle the arena, when she galloped right up in front of me and stopped. She stood as close to the gate as she could, just a little ways in front of me and turned her head all the way around. She looked me right in the eye, as if to say, *"Come on. What are you waiting for?"*

I didn't waste any time. I climbed over the rail onto her back, hung on, and away we went. Starburst wasn't wearing any tack, not even a halter. I didn't need it. I hung onto her mane and held tight. She reared up a couple of times but she wasn't trying to throw me. It was her way of letting me know she was having fun. After circling the arena a few times, a stable hand opened the gate and Starburst and I headed out into the sunshine.

Mom told me later that she knew Starburst and I belonged together when she saw us riding out from behind the farmhouse together, with no saddle and no bridle. It was the mutual trust between us that bonded us together.

So now, here it was November, a year later, and I was lying in my bedroom at our new house in Ohio, and Starburst was back at home in North Carolina, boarding with friends of ours. I was lonely. I wanted nothing more than to be healthy and have my horse. It seemed impossible, but I prayed anyway for there to be a way God could bring Starburst and I together again.

No one was happier than I was when, a few weeks later, a four-wheel-drive truck pulling a horse trailer pulled into our lane. It was Radonna, our friend who boarded our horse, and Margaret, her daughter. Starburst was in that horse trailer!

I was too sick to ride, but I went out and sat on Starburst. I wanted her to know I missed her and still loved her. She seemed to walk extra gently with me on her back, so I knew she understood what I was going through. It hurt my heart that I couldn't really ride her, but at least we were together. We kept Starburst in a fenced-in pasture next door. She had plenty of room to run, and Tyler, my younger brother, made sure she always had fresh water and hay.

By now, I had been in treatment for several weeks and felt lousy. Pain from my illness prevented me from going outside every day. The medication I was taking made me feel hot and sweaty all the time. I kept my bedroom window open at night, even though it was snowing outside. Lying with my head at the end of the bed to breathe in the cold, night air was the only thing that made me feel better.

One night, in the pitch-black darkness, something woke me. I wondered if I was dreaming. *Could this be?* It was Starburst! She was standing outside my opened window and put her face inside where I was lying. I could feel her breath on my cheek as she nuzzled me. I fell asleep like that.

In the morning, Tyler found Starburst standing out in the yard, rather than inside the fenced pasture. He and Mom couldn't find where she had gotten out – there was no visible opening in the fence and the gate was still locked. They put her back in and shrugged it off.

The next night, the same thing happened – Starburst came to me in the night. I fell asleep with her face next to mine. In the morning, I heard Mom and Tyler talking again about Starburst. "How did she get out?" I heard one of them ask.

Starburst's visits continued throughout the winter, the whole time I was in treatment. We never did figure out exactly how she escaped the confinements of the pasture. If you ask me, God's angel let her out because He knew I needed her, and He cares for me, as the Bible says. *"Casting all your cares upon Him; for He careth for you."* 1 Peter 5:7. ❧

Jacinda Gore, 2010
Sarasota, FL

❧ Compiler's Note: Jacinda struggled valiantly for life and health, always hoping for a miracle, but her struggle ended on Feb. 6, 2015, when she met her Bridegroom face to face. She is deeply missed by her family, who reside in Sarasota, Florida.

33

The Miracle-Working Nurse

"And when we cried unto the Lord, He heard our voice, and sent an angel..." Numbers 20:16

It was September, 2005, and we had arrived back from the United States only a few days before, after being there on furlough for almost two months. It had been three years since we had been in the States, and we had driven all the way from Belize to Kentucky to visit Dan's family; then west to see my family in Oregon before returning the many miles to Belize.

(Belize was home to us since 2001, when the handful of small church groups in the Toledo District had asked Dan to come down and start a high school for the Maya-Kekchi believers. Dan loved teaching, and it was a ministry close to his heart, to be involved in working with youth.)

It had been a long, difficult trip for me, and I was relieved when we arrived home. It was Dan's first day back in the class room for the year. But I didn't feel well enough that morning to get out of bed to wave him off.

Prior to the trip, I had been extremely sick for a couple of months because I was expecting a baby. I had terrible headaches and hardly slept and I knew my body was fighting against the unborn child. After every baby, I needed a Rhogam shot. But after Michael, our 21-month-old, was born, the local Cayo hospital would not give me the much-needed shot, as they were unfamiliar with it. While in the States, I lost the baby and instantly felt better physically. But now that I was back, I needed to have a D&C surgical procedure performed.

The children were sleeping, so I stayed in bed. After a while, I heard them get up so I got them breakfast, but then lay back down. Later, when I came down again, I almost fainted. I knew something was really wrong! I glanced around to see where my five children were. Baby Michael was sitting on the table and seven-year-old Abby, my oldest, was trying to take care of him. Rick, five, and Brendan, three, were sitting on the porch, and six-year-old Bryon was nearby.

I sat on the couch, and told Byron to get the old bike out of the shop. Dan had told them they couldn't ride it until they bought new spokes for it or it would bend the rim. I had no radio, no phone, and no vehicle! I told Byron to go to the neighbors and have them come and get me, and take me out to Dan, then on into town.

I couldn't lie down, because if I did, I couldn't breathe. So I sat there and prayed out loud, asking God to please help me stay alive, and also that I would get help! The neighbors soon came, and helped me into the vehicle. It was arranged that one of the neighbor girls would stay with the children. I dreaded to go because I was sure that this was the last time I would see my children.

We went to Dan's school and he got into the vehicle and took me to Jericho Road Clinic. But they said, "Go to a hospital, it's too serious. We can't deal with it here!"

So we rushed on to the government hospital in Punta Gorda, where they took me in and checked me out. They immediately got some IV drips and tried to find a vein. I don't know how many times they tried to get a vein, but couldn't find any! I was just too low on blood. (I needed a blood transfusion, but when I told them my blood type was O-negative, they said Belize didn't have blood banks for O-negative.)

The nurse in charge finally set everything down and told Dan to come to the nurses' station. I knew it had to be serious if she wouldn't say it in front of me. She told him the best thing to do would be to take me to a better hospital.

Soon after they went out, another nurse, dressed in white, came through the curtain. She had a happy, pleasant face. "So they didn't get your IV in yet?" she asked. I told her, no, that they had tried a lot and never got it in.

"I will pray and ask God to help me get this needle in," she said in Creole. After she had asked the Lord to help her, she picked up the needle and slid it in between my two smallest fingers on my right hand. I had never seen IV going in between a person's two small fingers before. It slid right in and started flowing. Ah! I felt a wave of relief go over me that maybe I would live.

The nurse said, "Everything will be alright," and disappeared about as quickly as she had come. I lay there, feeling so relieved, and prayed that all would go well.

Around five minutes later, the head nurse and Dan came in through the curtain to my bed. Noticing the IV solution flowing steadily into my hand, she asked in amazement, "Who put the IV in?" I told her about the friendly nurse who had just left.

The head nurse asked me, "Which direction did she go? What did she look like?" I tried to explain to her, so she disappeared out of the room to look. Soon she came back.

"I can't find anyone like you are describing! I don't know whom you are talking about," she told us.

Well, who was it? We couldn't exactly answer except that we knew God was there! He had answered our prayers when all hope seemed lost and the hospital staff had given up. The IV fluids gave me the boost I needed to stay alive!

In an hour, I was on the plane going to Belize City to a private hospital to have a D&C surgery. When I went in to surgery, they told me they did not have my blood type but would do the best they could. So they gave me lots of fluid and iron shots. Everything went well, and Dan and I were able to return home in five days and had a happy reunion with our children.

This story would have ended differently if God had not had mercy on us, sending this angel-nurse who knew just what to do! The fact that she didn't work there and no one knew her makes us feel certain that she was an angel on a heavenly mission.

In the hour that I thought I was not going to make it, I had prayed for my dear husband, my five children, my unsaved family, and most of all that I would be ready to meet God Almighty. I also told God that if I would live, I promised to remain faithful to whatever He called me to do. Years have passed, but I continue to ask myself, *"Am I keeping my promise?"* ❧

Lori Sullivan
Mafredi, Belize

❧ Compiler's Note: Dan & Lori are still living in Belize, and have made it their home. Since the time of this story, they were blessed with three more daughters, Shannon, Sarah and Carrie. Dan is still teaching at the high school. They built their own, small dairy farm for the children to work on, and also raise cacao trees.

34

The Praying Visitors

"Then the woman came and told her husband, saying, 'A man of God came unto me, and his countenance was like the countenance of an angel of God... but I asked him not whence he was, neither told he me his name...'" Judges 13:6

My wife, Eleanor, was at the Gettysburg, Pennsylvania, hospital following an operation, around 1963. The operation was successful, but she was feeling nauseated and could not keep any food down.

"Harold," the doctor said to me, "we cannot allow your wife to go home as long as she's nauseated like this. We can't release her until she has stabilized."

This went on and on, day by day. I would work during the day and visit her in the evenings. I prayed with her and read Scriptures, but nothing changed. We didn't know what else to do. She was receiving intravenous liquids to maintain her fluid levels and body weight, but her condition was not clearing up.

One evening, around a week after her operation, I went in to visit her and it was the same thing – no improvement. Before I left, we had prayer together. As I prepared to leave, I asked Eleanor, "Should I leave the door to your room open, or close it?" It was now after visiting hours.

"You may leave it open," Eleanor answered me, "the nurses will soon be here with my medication." So I left the door open and went back to our home, around six miles away.

The next day, Eleanor related this to me: "Harold, I heard you go down the hall, and your footsteps finally faded away. I lay back in bed, but about that time I heard steps coming down the hall."

Because the door was open, she kept watching the hall, and eventually, there came two, well-dressed men walking by the door. As they passed her door, one of them sprung back and said, "Eleanor!"

"Yes!" answered Eleanor. The men stepped into her room, and came over to her bed. She didn't know them, and had never seen them before.

"The Lord told us that there is someone here at the Gettysburg hospital that needs prayer," they said to her. Then they prayed a simple prayer, and soon left.

The next day, the hospital called and told me that she had dramatically improved. She was eating without vomiting anymore and was free to go home!

As I visited with her the following day about the amazing turn of events, we could only think of one possibility. "Harold," Eleanor said, "they could have been angels. They knew my name!"

How many times has the Lord intervened when it would appear that all hope was gone? ❧

Harold Miller, 2015
Hanover, PA

35

Waiting for the Angels

"And I beheld, and I heard the voice of many angels round about the throne... and the number of them was ten thousand times ten thousand, and thousands of thousands..." Revelation 5:11

T he phone rang. It was my niece Kimberly calling. "We're going to come over and visit Grandma. I'm so afraid that I won't get to tell her *goodbye*." As the oldest grandchild, and having grown up across the street from her grandmother, Kimberly felt very close to her. And now that Mom had suffered a stroke and was lying in bed, Kimberly wanted to come the four hours from South Boston, Virginia, to see her. "I will bring supper," she added.

After the Sunday morning church service, Kimberly made a quick lunch for her husband and five children, and then they got on the road to come see us, arriving around 5:00 p.m. She walked in with a big basket full of food for supper. "Could you put supper on?" she asked me. "I'm going to go visit with Grandma."

She had brought songbooks along, too. So, after eating supper, we sat around Mom's bed and sang for her. "Grandma said that she lies in bed and looks at the corner of the room, waiting for the angels to come," Kimberly told me. Mom had never told me that, and I felt a little hurt that I was the one taking care of her, yet she had never told me about looking for the angels.

So the next day, I said, "Mom, Kimberly told me that you look in the corner for the angels, waiting for them to take you home. Which corner?"

"Over there," she answered, staring to one corner of the bedroom. After that, I noticed that she gazed in that corner at times.

Mom rapidly and progressively declined, day by day. My sister, Naomi, from Mexico, came the following week and was a tremendous help in caring for her. On Thursday, Jan. 29, Mom had a massive stroke, and was no longer able to swallow, talk or communicate. I knew she was thirsty, but the corners of her mouth had turned down so far that anything I gave her would run out. I took a medicine dropper and tried squeezing in juice, but it would run out, or she would begin coughing since she couldn't swallow.

I felt so bad! I would ask, "Mom, do you want something to drink?"

"Mmmm," she would answer, looking at me with pleading eyes. I knew she was thirsty, and it broke my heart.

"Mom, you can't swallow." But she kept looking at me as though she wanted something, so I put water in a spray bottle and sprayed that in her mouth to give her some moisture.

On Saturday, she took a dip down, and her blood pressure dropped and was very low for about 24 hours. In the afternoon, I was by her bedside, along with my niece, Wilma, and we saw that she was getting weaker. Her body was shutting down, and she was lying there with her eyes closed, just trying to breathe. All of a sudden, her eyelids opened and she looked over in the corner, staring wide-eyed. She wasn't responding to us and was too weak to smile, but she just continued staring intensely toward the corner of the room.

"Mom! What do you see," I asked, *"tell us!"* But she wouldn't answer. After I left the room, my niece, Wilma, tried again to get a response. (Living nearby, she had often helped care for her grandmother, and there was a special bond between them.)

"Grandma, what do you see?"

"The angels," she answered weakly. Those were Mom's last words. She died the following day, on Feb. 1, 2015. I know the angels that were in the room carried her *home*, where she is so happy and free from suffering.

Mom left a hole that no one can fill, and the months following have been filled with sadness. I will always treasure the last months with her, serving her, crying with her, laughing with her, and even planning her funeral together. I miss her. But I look forward to being with her again, praising Jesus, with thousands of angels all around. ✎

Sarah Joy Beiler, 2015
Sarasota, FL/Belhaven, NC

✎ Compiler's Note: Just over seven months after her mother died, Sarah Joy's father, Solomon Beiler, also entered the presence of Jesus, on Sept. 26, 2015, at the age of 90.

Holy Ground

When I walked through the door, I sensed His Presence,
And I knew this was a place where love abounds,
For this is a temple, Jehovah, God, abides here,
And we are standing in His Presence on holy ground.

In His Presence there is joy beyond measure
And at His feet peace of mind can still be found,
If you have a need, I know He has the answer,
Just reach out and claim it
For you are standing on holy ground.

We are standing on holy ground,
And I know that there are angels all around;
Let us praise Jesus now, we are standing
In His Presence, on holy ground! - Geron Davis

36

Whisper of Wings

"Bless the Lord, ye His angels that excel in strength, that do His commandments, hearkening unto the voice of His word." Psalm 103:20

Beyond the jagged shadow of Mount Chile, the pale moonlight spilled over a slab-wood house securely shuttered against the night. The missionaries always carefully bolted every shutter at dusk, and securely barred the metal-reinforced door, every night. And certainly, every door and window was secured at twilight after the assassins threatened Ernest Helmuth, and after robbers broke into the house while the children were home alone. Yet, tonight, the door stood ajar.

Far in the distance, tail lights glowed like a pair of gleaming eyes, winking and then vanishing into the night. In the tattered shadows of the tropical trees sheltering the bungalow, a porch swing sighed and moaned in the darkness. In the pallid light of the moon, one could see the silhouette of a girl huddled in the corner of the swing.

A faint sniffling punctuated the stillness now and then. Overhead, a soft fluttering stirred the air – like the rustling of the breeze through the fronds of the tall coconut trees – or, perhaps, the whisper of an angel's wings.

Who cares if the door is unbolted, Christine thought. *Who cares if it stands ajar! Mama and the baby are dying!*

In the speeding pickup, the young girl's mother lay sprawled across the foam mat, feeling as though she was sinking into the darkness of death. She didn't have the energy to struggle, as the driver drove frantically over the rutted road toward the distant hospital, but waited complacently for the light at the end of the dark tunnel, knowing heaven was just beyond the blackness. The painful contractions, the bumpy road and endless retching were almost more than she could endure. Oh, to sink into the oblivion that threatened to swallow her.

Leaning over the back of the seat, Ernest held his wife's hand, brushed the hair form her damp forehead, talking to her, trying desperately to keep her from sinking into unconsciousness from which he sensed she would never awaken. "You've got to make it for the children, Virginia. You've got to fight." But she didn't respond.

How does it feel to die? the woman wondered. *Surely, going home to Jesus would be a lovely experience.* But then she thought of the children, of Ernest, and the load they would have to shoulder. *Oh, Lord, I have to survive for my family, and for the baby....*

As the lights of Tegucigalpa shone like tiny beacons, Ernest glanced at his watch. Two o'clock. *Only two hours,* he thought. *I wonder if anyone's ever driven from San Marcos to Tegucigalpa in less time.*

Ernest stumbled into the hospital with his wife in his arms. Nurses and orderlies rushed to her side, lifting Virginia onto a stretcher.

A nurse slapped on a blood pressure cuff, and pumped it vigorously. "I can't get any blood pressure," she cried.

"Start an IV!" the doctor barked.

"We've been trying, doctor, but we just can't find a suitable vein! Her blood vessels have all collapsed. It's too late!"

"There's not a soul in this hospital that could get a needle in a vein on that woman," another nurse agreed soberly. "Impossible. It's too late." The nurses turned away, leaving the body to be carted down to the morgue.

"Do something!" Ernest cried after them. "She's dying!" *Lord Jesus! Save my wife!*

Suddenly, a stocky Honduran nurse stood at Virginia's side. "Get a mariposa (butterfly needle)," she ordered with a quiet air of authority. "You must use a thinner needle, and stick it in above her elbow."

Deftly, the thin needle with its butterfly-shaped adapter was inserted into Virginia's upper arm, and the life-giving fluid dripped down the tube into her veins. With the fluid flowing through the veins, the blood vessels filled out enough that an IV needle could be stuck into the opposite hand as well. But Virginia never felt the prick.

"She's going to need blood," the doctor informed Ernest. "A lot of it. I'll have to see if we have any pints of A-positive blood on hand."

"Oh no, doctor," Ernest exclaimed. "That's a mistake! I know for a fact my wife's blood type is A-negative."

They'll kill her yet! he thought. *What if I couldn't speak Spanish?*

"Ah, well, maybe it is A-negative," the doctor agreed. "Okay, we'll have to check and see if we have any of that type on hand."

As the clear fluid dripped into her vein and pulsed through her body, Virginia stirred.

"Ah, Virginia, you are still with us," her husband murmured, observing the flutter of her eyelashes.

Glancing up, he saw the doctor striding in their direction. Suddenly, Ernest realized the physicians were the only other men in the room. *They're going to chase me out,* he realized. *Well, I won't go. Virginia can't understand much Spanish. I've got to stay.*

"Mr. Helmuth," the doctor looked up from his clipboard. "Once we perform a C-section, the bleeding will stop, but we've got to have more blood before we can operate. You'll have to quickly locate several units."

Ernest's eyes seemed to pierce the doctor. "You're telling me that I have to leave my wife and go find blood?"

"Why, yes, of course. We don't have enough, so you'll have to locate several units."

"And just where do I find blood?"

"Someone will tell you, but now you'll have to leave. Men aren't permitted in this labor room," the doctor announced decisively as he strode toward the next cot.

Just how am I supposed to find a donor at 4:00 on Saturday morning? Ernest wondered, as the hospital doors clanged shut behind him and he walked out into the night. *If I confront some man on the street this time of the night, he's likely to pull a knife on me. And if he doesn't mug me, would I even want blood for my wife from some character roaming the street at this hour?*

As the hours passed, the fog about Virginia began to lift. *I'm bleeding to death,* she realized as panic clawed at her heart. *I'm bleeding to death, and not a soul in this room cares.*

"Do something!" she pled with the staff that wandered past her bedside from time to time. "I'm dying!" But the nurses turned their backs and walked away.

"Please! A basin! I need to vomit!" Virginia called, gesturing to explain the broken Spanish words.

"Just lean your head over the side and vomit onto the floor," the nurse replied casually, as she bustled on by. And so, Virginia reluctantly turned her face to the side and retched out onto the floor.

The baby lay like a heavy weight on her spine. Virginia's legs and back throbbed with pain as she lay on the hard, unpadded table, and the contractions were merciless. Under the thin sheet, her entire body shook from shock.

After a frustrating, fruitless search, desperation welled within Ernest as he trudged wearily down the hospital hall. The light from the sun rising behind the mountains bled through the windows. *"Almost 6:00,"* he sighed, glancing at his watch. *"We've been here almost four hours."*

As a cluster of hospital staff stood quietly discussing the desperate situation, a doctor stepped out of surgery in time to hear the words: " ... haven't located any blood for the *gringa (white lady)* yet. It's absolutely amazing she's still alive."

"Say," the surgeon called, striding up to the huddle. "I'll donate a unit. I'm type O."

"Ah, type O! A universal donor!"

"How ... how kind of the surgeon to offer his blood ... " Ernest stammered, when approached about the offer, "But ... but ... I would like it tested first for hepatitis and AIDS."

"Testing is totally unnecessary," the physician said as he patted the surgeon's well-rounded stomach. "See how fat he is? You can tell by looking at him that he's nice and healthy. We won't be testing his blood. Besides, there isn't time. Here." He thrust a sheaf of papers at Ernest. "Here, sign on this line giving us permission to give your wife untested blood. Be quick about it, she's dying, after all."

The missionary lifted his eyes toward the ceiling. *God, will this nightmare never end?* With a shaking hand, he signed, *Ernest Helmuth.*

Five hours after her arrival at the Hospital Escuela, Virginia was wheeled into surgery.

"I'm so sorry, Virginia," Ernest apologized to his wife, holding her hand as he walked beside the stretcher on the way to the operating room. "I signed the papers for them to give you untested blood. I'm ter…." his voice broke. "I'm terribly sorry. But there was nothing else to do."

Virginia squeezed his hand. "It's okay, Ernest," she whispered. "It's either die now, or perhaps, die later. Besides, it's all in God's hands."

In what seemed to be weeks later, Virginia began to cough, and the searing pain of the fresh incision woke her from her anesthetic drowsiness as she lay on the gurney in the recovery room.

Slowly, she brought her shaky hand to her painful abdomen. Her hand touched only air where her stomach should have been, and floated slowly down until it touched her flattened abdomen. *The baby! Where's my baby?!*

"Por favor, quiero ver mi niño," Virginia begged the nurses in broken Spanish as they wheeled her to her room. "Please, I want to see my baby." But the nurses only shrugged and walked away.

They don't want to tell me, she thought. *Actually, have I felt any movement since that last flutter at the house?*

When Ernest walked into the room, he could tell that Virginia knew. "She was a lovely baby," he told her. "She had dark hair and a round face… just looked like she was sleeping… but she wouldn't breathe. And her lips were so dark purple. The doctor said that was a sign of her suffocating last night back when the hemorrhaging first started. That's what happens in placenta previa cases."

Why, God? What do you want to teach us?

Ernest glanced at this watch. The visiting hour was ending. "Oh, and what about a name? Do you still want to call her Emily?"

"I suppose." Virginia was too weary to care. She just wanted to sleep and sleep and sleep, and wake up to find it had all been an awful dream.

"Virginia."

"Yes."

"Where God has put a period, we dare not put a question mark."

She grabbed his strong, calloused, brown hand with her pale one. "I know, Ernest. I know. Somehow, God will see us through."

In the weeks that followed, there were many questions and hurts to work through. There were so many questions that plagued Virginia. *If God could miraculously spare my life, then why didn't He spare Emily's as well? Why did God allow our baby to die when we were giving our lives on the mission field? What do You want to teach us through this experience, Lord? What if... If only... Why?*

Though there seemed no clear answer to many of the questions, Virginia had an anchor.

"Have faith, trust Me," the Lord seemed to whisper as she clung to Him in the storm of grief. Gradually, she began to accept Emily's untimely death, trusting that someday she'd understand. And with the trusting acceptance came a quiet peace that filled the aching vacuum of her heart.

As the clock of time ticked on, the Helmuth family completed their term of service in Honduras, and moved back to the United States once again. Virginia packed away the blankets, booties and dresses, her heart stirring with the lonely ache as she thought of the shattered dreams and the tiny grave so far away. And then she thought of the new life growing within her – a new dream, a brand new hope.

When the local obstetrician questioned Virginia about her medical history, the story surfaced about the placenta previa, the massive blood loss and the two and a half hour trip to Tegus on bumpy, rutted roads.

"Mrs. Helmuth!" the doctor exclaimed. "Why, there is absolutely no medical reason to explain why you are alive today! Why, it's a wonder they could even find a vein in which to insert the IV needle!"

"They couldn't," Virginia smiled, thinking of the story she was about to share.

"They had given up on me. My veins had collapsed and no one could get an IV needle into any vein. In fact, they couldn't even get a blood pressure reading. Just when they were ready to give up, another nurse stepped up to my bed and told the staff to use a butterfly – a thinner needle – and to put it in above the elbow. The techniques worked and saved my life."

Virginia took a deep breath and continued. "Our friend's daughter-in-law was given the same bed I had used at Hospital Escuela. When the nurses found out she was from San Marcos, they asked if she knew the *gringa*, the white lady from San Marcos, who had just left the hospital."

Virginia paused momentarily, and then continued softly. "The nurses told our friend that after my crisis had passed, they looked around for the nurse that had suggested using a butterfly needle but no one could find her. "Who was that nurse?" they asked each other. She wore a hospital gown and looked like all the other Honduran nurses, but no one had ever seen her before … nor did they ever see her again. They all thought … "

"She was an angel!" the doctor burst out. "That nurse was an angel!"

"That's what they said at Hospital Escuela." Virginia's face was radiant.

"God was watching over you down in Honduras, Mrs. Helmuth," the doctor announced decidedly. "I could tell you of numerous placenta previa cases here in the United States, with its ambulances, EMTs and trauma centers, where mother and baby both died. Both of them."

Months later, the notes of a lullaby accompanied by the creaking of a rocking chair floated through the Helmuth home. Virginia glanced lovingly at the tiny head of dark hair nestled against the shoulder of her oldest daughter, Christine. A white shawl flowed down across her lap, and a corner of the shawl dropped to reveal a pastel, blue dress. How healing it was for Christine to hold the warm bundle close to her heart. Like a poultice, the infant seemed to draw the pain from deep within her chest, and erase the memories of that traumatic night, months earlier, when she had huddled in fear as her mother was taken away and rushed to the hospital.

Melody. What a fitting name, for she filled their hearts and home with a song once again.

At times, Virginia had struggled with the question of why God had spared her life and not her baby's. But once she discovered that God had sent an angel to her rescue, she could no longer question the purposes of such a mighty God. Just knowing He had sent an angel to save her life inspired Virginia to accept with all her heart, rather than pining away, wondering *why*, and thinking what might have been.

And Virginia knew when God's plan for her life on earth was completed the angels would carry her home to Heaven, where she'd see her precious Emily at last. Perhaps her darling would be waiting at the pearly gate with a kiss for her mother. Then, hand in hand, the two of them would search Heaven for the angel that came to the rescue that unforgettable night.

Ah, how a babe in Heaven drew one's heart toward Home beyond the skies. Yes, every day Virginia would keep listening, listening for the whisper of angel's wings. ❧

Dorcas Hoover
Dover, OH

❧ Compiler's Note: This story took place in San Marcos, Honduras, in 1993. Ernest and Virginia Helmuth now live in Kentucky, and Melody, the newborn in this story, married in May, 2015.

This condensed story is used by permission from the book *Whisper of Wings,* by Dorcas Hoover, available from the publisher, Carlisle Press, 2673 TR 421, Sugarcreek, Ohio 44681; 330-852-1900.

37

Crossing Dangerous Borders

"Let them be as chaff before the wind: and let the angel of the Lord chase them. Let their way be dark and slippery: and let the angel of the Lord persecute them." Psalm 35:5, 6

In the 1970s and 1980s, my parents, Dave and Amy Bontrager, were involved in a work which they had founded, *Jesus to the Iron Curtain*. They brought aid in the form of Bibles, medicines and other needed items to the suffering Christians in communist countries. These things had to be smuggled in, as the governments forbade the people to have Bibles.

On one of their trips, they were going through a line at the airport to have their luggage checked. They had forbidden items, like Bibles, in their luggage. They were praying every step of the way as they moved through the line.

Finally, it was their turn. As they stepped up to be checked, a man with the bluest of eyes came up to the other side of the counter and said, "You must come with me right away. The bus is waiting."

So the inspector waved them on through and they followed the man with the blue eyes to the outside of the building where the bus was indeed waiting. When Dave turned to thank the man, there was no one there!

They looked in every direction, including at the building, which had many large glass windows – but there was no one there! They got onto the bus, where they waited for about half an hour before taking off. They always believed God had sent an angel to help them in their time of need.

Part 2

O n another occasion, my parents were driving through Hungary to Romania. They had items in their possession that were forbidden behind the Iron Curtain. Traveling with them was a Christian sister from Germany.

As they drove along, this sister saw some dried weeds along the road that she thought were pretty. She wanted to stop and pick them. They had fluffy tops, something like those of dandelions going to seed. They decided it would probably be alright, so they stopped, picked them, and then laid them on top of a suitcase in the trunk.

They soon approached the border of Romania, which was the danger point. Knowing they had forbidden articles in one suitcase, they were apprehensive and were much in prayer. Driving up to the officer, they stopped and he began to question them. Then he told them to get out of the car as he began to search it. Next he told them to open the trunk. What were they to do? They opened the trunk, praying all the time.

There were two suitcases. Dave reached for the one that had their clothing in it, but the guard said, "No – I want to see inside *that* suitcase!" It was the one with the forbidden items. It was also the one with the dried weeds on top of it.

In his nervousness, Dave dropped the lid of the suitcase they had already opened, and the puff of air that the falling lid created swept through the dried bouquet, filling the air with flying fluff and downy seeds as the bouquet flew apart right in the officer's face. He began to sneeze violently. He was evidently allergic to the weeds.

As Dave apologized to him, he said, "I've seen quite enough. Just close your trunk and go!" So God protected them with a bouquet of dried weeds! ᴥ

Katie Slabaugh, 2014
Nappanee, IN

Roles of Angels – Bible Quiz

1. Angels *assist* us in witnessing for Jesus, as in the life of _____ (Acts 8:26-40) and in _____ conversion. (Acts 10:1-43)

2. Angels *carry* us to heaven, as in the life of _____. (Luke 16:22)

3. Angels *comfort* and *encourage* us, as in the life of _____. (Acts 27)

4. Angels *deliver* us, as in the life of _____. (Acts 12: 7-10)

5. Angels *destroy*, as warriors of God, as in the life of King _____, who was very proud and didn't give God the glory. (Acts 12:21-23)

6. Angels *give messages* to us, as in the life of _____ wife (Judges 13:1-21) and as in the life of _____. (Luke 1:26-35)

7. Angels *guard*, as in the lives of _____, keeping them from reentering the Garden of Eden (Genesis 3:24); and as in the life of _____. (Numbers 22:21-35)

8. Angels *lead* us and *direct* our way, as in the life of _____. (Genesis 15:2; Genesis 24:1-7)

9. Angels *provide food and water* for us, as in the life of _____. (1 Kings 19:5-7)

10. Angels *rejoice* when a _____ comes to repentance. (Luke 15:10)

11. Angels *strengthen* us in persecution and trials, as in the life of _____ (Luke 22:43, 44) in the garden of Gethsemane and after His temptation. (Matthew 4:11)

12. Angels *surround* and *protect* us, as in the life of _____ and his servant (2 Kings 6:15-17), and in the life of _____. (Daniel 6:22)

- Vera Overholt

38

"Get off the Road!"

"And the angel of the Lord called unto him out of heaven..." Gen. 22:11

One day, as my brother Elson and I were walking down our country road, heading for the neighbors, I suddenly heard an urgent voice beside me, saying, "Martha, get off the road!" Speeding up over the hill behind me, there appeared a red car.

I looked around, trying to determine where the voice might have come from. Seeing no one, I called Elson, who was now a distance ahead, to wait for me. When I caught up with him and told him what had happened, he said that he, too, had heard a voice that said, "Elson, get off the road!"

I have rehearsed this incident many times since it happened in 1946, and to this day, around 66 years later, I can still vividly see the car in my memory! As I think about this experience, I am always moved by this confirmation of my Father's love for His children, and the protection of His angels.

I am reminded of the verse in Psalm 91:11, *"He shall give His angels charge over thee, to keep thee in all thy ways."* &

Martha Sommers Gingerich, 2014
Mooresville, NC

&> Compiler's Note: My sister, Martha, and her husband, Al, live in North Carolina. They have four children and eleven grandchildren.

39

His Awesome Presence

"And the angel of His presence saved them...and He bare them, and carried them..." Isaiah 63:9

I t was just another usual day in Florida, in 2004. I decided to do my grocery shopping at two different stores. I liked to do my shopping in the forenoon, as the traffic was not as heavy then. I often breathed a prayer asking God's protection before starting out.

I had gone several miles when I sensed a very real Presence in the passenger seat of my minivan. I even turned my head to the right, but the seat was empty. My thoughts went heavenward and I pondered the meaning of it. I had never experienced a happening like this before. It did not scare me, but I felt a calmness wash over me.

I finished my shopping and made a stop at the bank on my way home. I headed west through Pinecraft, crossing the bridge, and got in the turning lane that goes into the Sara Lake neighborhood.

I slowed down, and then applied the brakes, but my brakes were gone! I managed to stop just before hitting the concrete that surrounds the median.

I decided to try to make it home and get off the busy highway, and crept along at a very slow speed. I was barely moving as I pulled into our carport and put the car in park.

As I was unloading groceries, a neighbor man came by and I shared my story. He got down to take a look and exclaimed, "No wonder you didn't have brakes. Your brake fluid line broke and is hanging down to the ground!"

Later, as I stepped into the house, I suddenly felt very weak when I thought of what all could have happened in that heavy traffic. Then I remembered the awesome Presence I had sensed on my way to the store. From the depths of my heart I thanked and praised God for sending His angel to protect me. ❧

Martha Hostetler, 2015
Linn, MO/Sarasota, FL

O for a thousand seraph tongues
To bless the incarnate Word!
O for a thousand thankful songs
In honor of my Lord!

– Charles Wesley

40

Lost!

"For there stood by me this night the angel of God, whose I am, and whom I serve." Acts 27:23

"Come, Petrona, it's time to start out for home," Catarina called to her daughter. "Hurry! The sun is halfway down the sky, and we want to be home before it gets dark."

The brown-skinned, Belizean woman tied her baby daughter, Juana, securely into the carrying-cloth on her back. "Thank you, and goodbye," she shyly told the nurse, who had just finished caring for both of her daughters at the clinic.

Reluctantly, Petrona left the group of children she had been playing with and followed her mother. It usually took about three hours to walk from the Crique Sarco Mission clinic back to her village of Otexa… a long, weary journey. But 9-year-old Petrona understood the need for haste. She, too, wanted to get home before darkness fell!

The afternoon was hot and humid. Soon droplets of sweat trickled down Catarina's face and neck. Baby Juana, fussy and fretful from the shot she had received at the clinic, whimpered uneasily until at last she fell asleep on her mother's back.

"I'm so thirsty, Mama!" Petrona began to complain. "When can I get a drink?"

"There will be a creek by the trail soon," Catarina replied. "You can take a drink there."

Silently, the three plodded along the path. Lush, green vines, trees and flowers flourished on all sides in the moist heat. Tropical orchards in every shade of pink, red and purple bloomed from the crannies of the older trees, while smaller trees bore wild fruits – coconuts, May plums and guavas. Bamboo canes grew thickly wherever they could find room, with their lovely sun-dappled leaves. A monkey called to his companion in the distance, and exotic birds flashed through the trees on business of their own.

But Catarina and Petrona scarcely saw the beauties of this wild bush country. Their minds were on their home and supper.

"I'm going to take this old short cut," Catarina suddenly announced. "We don't usually come this way. But it will save time!" Turning from the well-worn trail, she led Petrona off along another path. This trail looked like it had not been used very much in recent years. Vines and bamboo shoots were growing across the path, nearly hiding it from view.

"Now, we should be home sooner," Catarina said with satisfaction. Mother and daughter began to walk more briskly along the shady, overgrown trail. It was slightly cooler under the trees, but Catarina soon found that the old path was hard to follow. Sharp bamboo spears kept stabbing her bare feet, and sometimes the trail was blocked completely by fallen logs. Sometimes she wasn't even sure where the path was! But she plodded on, and Petrona silently followed.

It seemed like they had been walking for hours when suddenly the air darkened and a gust of wind whipped through the trees. "Mama, it's going to rain!" Petrona groaned.

Sure enough, great drops of rain began to fall. Soon the drops became a downpour, and the travelers left the trail to stand under a big tree. When the shower let up a little, Catarina was ready to leave their shelter and go on. "We have to hurry!" she worried. "It will soon be dark, and then I won't be able to see this trail!"

Baby Juana began to cry again as they trudged along through the drizzling rain. The path grew harder to find as the light faded slowly. Suddenly it came to an end, at the edge of a large open space.

"Mama, this looks like a cornfield!" Petrona exclaimed. "See, the old stubble is still standing in rows even though weeds are growing up in them."

"Yes, someone used to live around here, and this was their cornfield," Catarina agreed. "Now, where can the trail be?" Hurrying through the cornfield, she found the path once more on the other side... or was it the path?

Dusk was falling and it was hard to be sure. Maybe I should have stayed with the regular trail, Catarina thought fearfully. Hurrying, she forced her tired legs to move on.

"Mama, it's getting dark," Petrona spoke in a small voice.

"Yes, I know. Walk faster," was all her mother replied. Mosquitoes appeared in great clouds as the sun went down. Petrona waved her arms in all directions, quietly slapping the ones that zoomed in to land on her. There was no use complaining, she knew. All they could do was hurry, to get out of these woods before darkness brought snakes and jaguars out of their hiding places. Jaguars! Petrona shivered and moved faster.

Hungry, thirsty, and so tired, the three pushed on. When darkness fell, it was completely dark. There is no darkness on earth as black as the darkness of a tropical night in Belize, when rain clouds blot out the moon and stars! Bravely, Catarina kept on trying to find her way along the trail. Feeling with her hands and bare feet, she moved slowly through the dense jungle.

All at once, she stopped in surprise. "What is this?" she cried out softly. "It feels like ... "

"It's cornstalks, Mama," Petrona whispered. "We're in the cornfield again! How could we be?"

"We must have gone in a circle," Catarina groaned in despair. "We're lost. It's no use; I can't follow that old trail in the dark. All we can do is stay here and wait till morning!"

Feeling around for a smooth spot on the ground, Catarina and Petrona sat down close together. The mother lifted her baby from the carrying cloth on her back and cuddled her in her arms. Silently, the three sat listening to the sounds of the night: the whining mosquitoes, the faint crackling as a small animal moved close by, and the call of a night bird. Far away Petrona heard a cry, and fear prickled along her backbone. Could that have been a jaguar?

But Catarina was hearing something else. "Chug-chug-chug-chug...," sounded the distant rumbling of a motor.

"Listen!" she whispered. "Do you hear that, Petrona? It's the generator of Crique Sarco. The machine they use to make electric lights for the mission. We must not be too far away – maybe only two or three kilometers, straight over."

She stirred restlessly, slapping at a mosquito. "If we could just walk straight toward the sound ... " she said thoughtfully.

"Oh, Mama, no!" cried Petrona. "I'm so tired, and it's too dark to walk!"

Catarina sat in silence for a moment, considering. Then, abruptly, she made her decision. Rising to her feet, she placed the sleeping Juana in her older sister's lap. "I'll go by myself," she stated. "If I am alone, I can run. I will get to the mission quickly and bring back men with lights. We can spend the night at the mission, where we will be safe!"

Tears streamed down Petrona's cheeks. "Mama, don't go!" she whimpered.

"Yes, that will be the best way," her mother replied firmly. "You stay right here and don't make a sound. Try to keep Juana quiet, too, so nothing will...." she stopped. "Pray to God," she added softly, and vanished into the black night.

Through the darkness the desperate mother ran like a deer, her hands always outstretched before her to feel for trees and other obstacles that might block her way. Surely the noise she made as she crashed blindly through the bushes would scare away any snakes or jaguars that might be lurking there?

Straining her ears to hear that chug-chug-chug of the generator, she followed the sound. In the inky blackness of the night, there was no way to watch where she stepped! Many times, poor Catarina moaned with pain as a sharp bamboo shoot stabbed into one of her bare feet. Twice she tripped and fell headlong to the ground, but there was nothing to do but get up and keep going. She had to get help to find her children, and quickly!

The clock in the mission house showed 10:30 p.m. when Alvin Schlabach heard the knock on his door. There stood a woman he had seen at the clinic earlier in the day, but how different she looked now! Her dress was torn in several places, and her bare feet were bleeding from many cuts.

"Help me, Mr. Alvin!" Catarina cried tearfully. "My children are lost in the bush!"

Hastily the missionary led the tired woman to a chair while his wife, Irene, brought a fresh drink and bandages for her cut feet. After hearing Catarina's story, Alvin put on his boots and picked up his most powerful flashlight.

"I will get some men together, and we will go look for the girls," he assured Catarina. "You stay here. I will take Juan Choc along; he knows all the bush country around here. He will know exactly where that old cornfield would be!" Alvin turned to his wife. "Pray for us," he told her. With a smile and wave, he was gone.

In a very short time, the missionary had a group of men ready to go. There were two health workers from the clinic, the Belizean Christian, Juan Choc, and another man named Nicholas.

My, this is a black night, Alvin thought as he followed the beam of the flashlight Juan carried. *I would soon be lost myself if it weren't for Juan and the others!*

He pictured a little girl out in this darkness, alone except for her baby sister, and shuddered. *There are snakes out there, and vampire bats, and jaguars! Lord, please protect those poor children and help us find them soon,* he prayed silently.

Juan Choc was an expert hunter and tracker in the bush, and he followed the old, almost-invisible trail easily. By midnight, the men had found the cornfield. But the overgrown field was empty – only rows of dead stubble and weeds showed in the flashlights' beams.

"Petrona! Petrona, where are you?" the men called. They fanned out across the whole field, searching carefully for the missing children. Could the girls be asleep? What had happened?

"They aren't in this field," Juan announced, frustrated. "And this is the only field in the area. I don't know what to do now." He began to circle slowly around the field, looking for clues.

"Petrona! Where are you, Petrona?" Alvin called. "Petrona!" shouted the other men.

Suddenly, out of the distant blackness came an answering call. "Over here!"

"That was a man's voice, not a child's!" Alvin exclaimed. "Who else would be out here on such a night?"

"Who's there?" Juan shouted.

Again the voice answered faintly. "Over here!"

Out of the cornfield and through the bush, Alvin and his friends followed the strange voice. Whenever they called, the man's voice would reply. Keeping alert for snakes, the five searchers pressed through the thick bamboo and vines.

"Over here! Come this way!" the strange voice sounded closer. "The children are here!"

"Who do you suppose he is?" Alvin asked Nicholas. "It sounds like he has found the girls!"

"I don't know, but we will find out in a moment," the other man replied. "We're almost there."

"Over here!" the voice called one last time, and then there was a silence, followed by the sleepy wail of a baby.

"Petrona! Juana!" Alvin shouted.

"Here I am!" came a small, frightened voice. Swinging his powerful light toward the sound, Juan saw the children at last. Huddled on the ground under a tree, Petrona still held her baby sister in her arms. Both children were speckled with mosquito bites, cold and sleepy and thirsty – but safe.

Gently, Alvin picked up the baby. "How did you girls get so far away from the cornfield?" he asked Petrona.

"I thought I heard a jaguar," the girl confessed. "I was scared, and I just ran till I couldn't go anymore."

"Where's the man who was with you?" Juan demanded, shining his light through the trees.

"There wasn't anyone else with me," Petrona answered sleepily, clinging to the missionary's friendly hand. "Not any man at all!"

"But we heard a man calling," Nicholas insisted. "Where are you?" he shouted. The other man called repeatedly, but there was no reply.

"Nobody's here," said Juan at last. "But we all heard his voice. Do you think…" he stopped.

In the silent darkness, a feeling of awe and reverence swept over Alvin. Surely, God was near! "It must have been an angel," he spoke softly. "God sent an angel to protect the children and to be with them until they were found." ❧

Mildred Martin
Mifflin, PA

❧ Author's Note: This story happened near Crique Sarco, Belize, in 1992. Catarina, Petrona and Juana spent a few days at the clinic to have their bites and cuts treated, and then the missionaries took them safely home to their own village. Alvin Schlabach was an American missionary pastor in Crique Sarco at the time of this story. He and his wife, Irene, had been in Belize for just a year when this incident happened. They are now living in Dade City, Florida.

From *Missionary Stories with the Millers*. Used by permission.

41

Lost in a Tokyo Hotel

"... The angel...talked with me..." Zechariah 1:9

In 1968, my wife, Maddy, and I were returning from Manila, Philippines, for furlough in the United States. We were traveling with our five children, Paul, Tim, Marilyn and our 2-month-old twin girls. I carried one of the twin babies and my briefcase with the money, tickets and travel documents. Paul carried the toy bag and led his little 2-year-old sister, Marilyn. Maddy had the diaper pail and the other twin.

We flew from Manila to Japan, via Hong Kong, on our way back to the United States. Our plane was delayed leaving Hong Kong, so we didn't arrive in Tokyo until after midnight. We arrived dead tired from that leg of our journey. The travel agent had booked us into the twelve-story New Otani Hotel, one of the largest in that city of fourteen million people.

Upon arriving, I went to the desk in the foyer to get checked in and get our room key. Maddy was with me, watching the babies and the other two children. All of a sudden, we saw 6-year-old Paul at the far side of the foyer, pushing elevator buttons. He had never been in an elevator before and was interested to see how they worked. Before we could say a word, an elevator door opened and he disappeared inside.

We quickly rushed down, expecting him to step out when the elevator arrived back again on the floor. The elevator came back down – but no Paul! It was empty. Now, you can imagine our consternation. We were in the huge city and couldn't speak Japanese. The man at the counter spoke hardly any English. This hotel had hundreds and hundreds of rooms, and we had a boy lost at 1:00 in the morning.

I took Maddy and the rest of the children up to our room, No. 53 on the seventh floor, then decided to go out to hunt for Paul. In the meanwhile, we were praying hard for wisdom and guidance, as well as for our own composure.

I deposited the family in the assigned room and then turned back to the elevators on that floor to go and look for Paul. I barely got to the doors when the elevator opened – and out walked little Paul!

I asked him how he knew that he was to get out on the seventh floor. "A man in the elevator told me to get out on this floor," he replied.

Now think about this. Only the man at the check-in counter knew to which room we were assigned. There was no one else around when we checked in. And yet a man who could speak English "happened to be" in that elevator and knew that Paul was to get off on the seventh floor.

Do I believe in miracles? Do I believe in angels being with us unawares? (Hebrews 13:2) Yes, I do! This is just one of those many instances where we saw the Lord working in marvelous ways in our lives as we worked for Him and the Kingdom of Glory. ❧

Les Troyer

❧ Compiler's Note: Paul, the little boy in this story, was born in the Philippines, where his parents were missionaries for many years. Later, they served in Nepal for five years. Wanting to include this story, but not knowing how to locate Paul, I put a notice in *The Budget* newspaper (a weekly publication of news from Amish-Mennonite communities around the world). To my surprise, I found out that he lives right here in Sarasota, Florida, not far from us!

Taken from *Speak, Lord, for Thy Servant Heareth*, by Robert J. Yoder. Used by permission.

42

Miracle Hannah

"And when we cried unto the Lord, He heard our voice, and sent an angel…"
Numbers 20:16

It was an unusually warm day for mid-December in southwestern Missouri, and we were enjoying part of the afternoon outdoors. But towards evening, the wind abruptly turned colder and storm clouds appeared in the sky. It began raining heavily and the temperature dropped to 40°. We discussed cancelling our evening plans of going to our friends' place, where the young people were gathering for supper and the singing afterward, but then decided to keep our plans and go.

After we arrived by horse and buggy at Gideon Bontrager's home, it rained again, and everything was becoming icy as the temperature continued to drop. We enjoyed our evening, but were feeling uneasy about the storm front moving in.

Around 9:30, as we were preparing to go home, I heard someone say it was 22°. It was very windy and cold as we went outside to leave. My husband, Reuben, stepped back from our horse and lifted three-year-old Hannah into the buggy, and then he turned around to get the baby, Rose Ann, from me. Just then, the horse started to move. Though normally very safe, he was cold and in a hurry to get home.

"Whoa!" called Reuben, and the horse stopped, but only for an instant. As Reuben turned again to get Rose Ann, the horse took off! Reuben ran after the buggy and threw himself into the passenger side to grab the lines. But just as he touched them, the back wheels caught his legs and pulled him to the ground, and ran over both of his knees.

Reuben jumped up and yelled at Junior, a friend who was walking home, to stop the horse. As the horse came up to him, Junior tried to catch him but the horse jumped to the side, narrowly avoiding being caught.

Reuben immediately rushed to the shop to alert the youth boys who had gathered there after the singing, and he and some of the boys took off running after the buggy.

As the buggy went out of sight, we heard the pitiful screams of little Hannah. Oh, what a helpless, heart-wrenching feeling, as I stood there and could not do a thing about it!

When Reuben and the other boys got to the neighbor's place where my unmarried brother, William, had parked his buggy, they quickly hitched up his horse to chase our runaway horse and buggy. Some others kept on running after it. As it turned the corner at Highway P, a two-lane county road, it hit the culvert at the side, jolting the buggy, and Hannah was thrown out on the road. By the time the boys, on foot, arrived at that corner only a few minutes later, Hannah had already disappeared. She must have jumped up right away and ran in the opposite direction.

Not realizing she had been thrown out, the boys continued running after the horse and buggy, which was speeding toward home. Meanwhile, Reuben caught up with it and followed closely behind. When the horse went on past our lane, my brother jumped out, ran up alongside and jumped in. But to his shock and dismay, Hannah was no longer in the buggy! He quickly informed Reuben.

How is that possible? Reuben's thoughts were churning. *Our horse and buggy have been within sight all of the time, and we have been watching the ditches in case she would fall out!*

Immediately, the men turned around and started searching both sides of the road on the way back, but not a trace of Hannah was found. I was anxiously waiting at the Bontragers' home when they returned with the bad news. *Oh, where can our little girl be?* My hope plummeted. *How can she survive being out on this stormy night?* It was bitterly cold with a strong wind blowing.

My younger sister, Kristina, and I went home in her buggy, searching ditches as we went, but to no avail. By then, the young folks, and all who knew about our lost child, were out searching with spotlights and flashlights, braving the elements. The sheriff's department had been called, and within an hour after the runaway, dozens of people were helping to search.

It was a miserable night to be out. It had started sleeting, and everything became white and slippery. By midnight, the temperature had dropped to 10° with the wind chill around 0°. Hannah had already been missing for over two hours. My mother and sisters and I were staying overnight at the home of our friend, Miriam, waiting and praying. *Lord, please keep her safe. Please help her to be found soon!*

My father and brothers were out with the men, assisting in the search efforts, but the law officers wanted Reuben to stay with them. As the search continued, word of the missing little girl traveled fast, and more and more people arrived to help. By midnight, the sheriffs estimated that around 150 people were helping to comb the area. They searched in every building, culvert, field and any place they thought she might be. Everything was searched again and again and yet not a trace of Hannah could be found! Our hearts were breaking. *Will we ever see her smile or hear her talk again?*

The night wore on. At 4:00 in the morning, the search party met at the church house which was being used as the command center, on Highway P. The sheriff assigned a representative from each search group to go into another room to strategize their next course of action. Reuben and the church leaders were also in that meeting. The difficult decision was finally made to call off the organized, grid searches until daybreak, since they had done all that they could.

Although the grid search was on hold, many people went on searching informally until daybreak. Rescue workers with search dogs were also helping until 5:00 a.m. Miriam, with the help of other women, made breakfast for the cold, weary bunch.

It had been a long, sleepless night for those of us waiting. Reuben had been checking in on me throughout the night with the latest updates. *Where is our daughter? Why hasn't she been found?* We wrestled with questions, weary from exhaustion and disappointment. *Is it her appointed time to be called home?*

At 6:30, as the gray and cloudy morning dawned, everybody gathered once more at the church house to organize another large grid search. We women watched from Miriam's house as the huge search party started out once more, forming a long line of men, side by side. Suddenly, we saw the men running towards the church house! *What was happening?*

We waited in suspense for several minutes, and soon found out that someone had yelled that Hannah had been found and she was alright! Oh, what a miracle! Tears of relief and thankfulness overwhelmed me. *She's alive! Thank you, God!*

Someone came at once and took my mother and me to the church house, where Hannah was sitting, surrounded by the search and rescue team. Reuben was already at her side. Words cannot express our feelings as we held our little girl once again! We had never given up hope that she would be found, but we didn't know if she would be found alive. We listened in amazement as Linda Banks, the local woman who found her, told us her story.

That Monday morning, Linda had heard on the news that little Hannah was lost, so she wanted to go to work a little earlier in case they might be able to find her. As she scanned the roadsides on her way to work, something caught her attention. From a distance, it looked like a garbage bag, but she asked her husband to stop anyway, and ran back to check it out. It was the lost little girl! Her face was tucked under her black shawl. Linda quickly reached under the shawl and touched her face, shocked to feel that it was still warm and little Hannah was sleeping! She quickly picked the child up and ran back to the truck. Hannah started crying, asking for *"Mom."*

Hannah didn't have a shoe on her right foot and it was very swollen. But amazingly, she had no frostbite. Hannah's knees were bruised from falling off of the buggy, and she had a black and blue mark on her right leg where she said the buggy wheels went over her. Other than being cold, that was the extent of her physical injuries! She had been in that bitter cold, wind and sleet for almost ten hours, without thick underclothes. And her outer wraps were only a coat, shawl and bonnet. When they took off her shawl, there was sleet between her coat and shawl. When Reuben first saw her and took hold of her hand, he said it was not as cold as it usually was when she would go out to do the chores with him. And when her temperature was taken after the ambulance arrived, it was almost 97° – amazing!

In the back of the ambulance, Hannah told me her story, as we sped to Aurora-St. John's hospital, fifteen minutes away. She had leaned forward to get the lines to stop the horse, but then she fell out of the buggy and the wheel went over her leg. Then she followed the white road. *Which white road did she follow?* She said she was crying and kept calling for us, but we didn't hear, and she couldn't understand where we were. *Reuben called her name frequently while searching, but with the strong wind she did not hear him,* I realized. She recounted how she saw a house, but didn't want to go in, but slept on the grass beside the road. She said she saw a lot of Christmas lights. *That was probably the flashing lights on the police and rescue vehicles. She calls all bright lights "Christmas lights."* She recalled how she was afraid of the cars that went past her and the men that came close to her while she was lying there. *Oh, how nearly she was discovered,* my thoughts were racing. *God didn't intend for us to find her last night.* She told me she lost her shoe, and when it came off, she couldn't put it back on. She said it sleeted and snowed on her after she lay down. I held her hand tightly as she related the incredulous details, in awe of God's protection.

Hannah was released from the hospital around noon that day. She didn't even get a cold from her night out in the freezing, cold weather! And she had no frostbite, though she was not far from it – the skin on her right toes peeled off a few weeks later. Her missing shoe was found where she had been lying, in a shallow ditch beside a culvert near Highway 39, about half a mile from where she had been thrown.

Later, we learned that a police officer said he saw a glimpse of an angel during the night, while searching in the field close to where she lay. We have no doubt that a guardian angel had his warm, protecting hand over her during that long night. And we never fully realized the depth of a miracle until one happened to us. ❦

Edna Yoder, 2009
Verona, MO

❧ Compiler's Note: This miraculous event happened on December 14, 2008, impacting the entire community in a way that would not soon be forgotten, and bringing glory to the One who still performs miracles today! Eight years later, Hannah is a happy, healthy girl, living with her family on their farm in Verona, Missouri. Since this story took place, she has four additional siblings.

43

Rescued!

"...Now I know of a surety, that the Lord hath sent His angel, and hath delivered me..." Acts 12:11

One winter, weekday morning, as hectic as any other New York City morning, I descended hurriedly into a subway platform as part of my daily, work commute. I quickly worked my way through the crowds in order to be close to an open door of the next train.

Thus, I found myself on the edge of the platform as one pulled into the station. I waited for the doors to open and prepared to board, as I had routinely done so many times before. But the ensuing moments would be a radical departure from my typical experience.

A veritable, human avalanche-in-waiting had gathered around and about me in the intervening moments, and another one pressed against the doors from within the train. Now the doors opened, and the disembarking passengers surged forward. I was pushed off balance and sent sprawling to the hard cement. To my shock and dismay, one of my legs was lodged between the platform's edge and the momentarily resting train.

The conductor was unaware of my plight, and would soon close the doors and give the okay for departure. All frantic efforts to regain my footing were futile, as the ceaseless collision of those elbowing their way from the train and those energetically stampeding ahead prevented any remedy. My heart was clouded by visions of a crushing injury to be inflicted by the soon-to-depart train, and a fall to the electrified tracks below.

But then, just seconds before the conductor pushed the close-door button and the train hurtled off, a pair of hands skillfully reached through the tumult and slipped under my arms. The grip was instantly secured and I found myself being lifted without impediment out of danger and to my feet. I turned quickly to express my gratitude to my benefactor. All there was to see was the back of a blue-coated, black-hatted man moving hurriedly away. In seconds, he was gone.

The grace of God had certainly visited me that day, and in a most peculiar way. The strangeness of my rescuer's sudden and silent appearance and disappearance was most odd. His skill and effortless efficiency were remarkable.

And then there was this: How did he notice my predicament? If he was not initially in close proximity he would have required uniquely keen perception to see through the trampling throngs. If he had been exiting the nearby train door we would have been facing each other, and I would have surely noticed his approach. It is then quite likely that he would have stayed by my side long enough to satisfy any doubts as to my wellbeing. "Are you alright?" is a question I would have expected to hear.

On the other hand, if he had been rushing to enter the train, he would have continued to do so after engaging in his noble act. Instead, he turned and moved toward the station's exit. And so, upon later reflection, it occurred to me that perhaps God had resolved my plight by dispatching an angelic friend. ≈

Elda Curdumi Mason, 2014
Dayton, VA

≈ Compiler's Note: This story happened around 1999.

44

"Run!"

"... In heaven their angels do always behold the face of my Father which is in heaven." Matthew 18:10

It was a breezy, June evening in the summer of 2015, and the birds were singing on our farm in Tennessee, where we were working for a short time. Although we live in Florida, we travel there quite often in preparation for moving someday, and our farm is a work in progress.

My husband, Nathan, and I were at work in the barn, and it would soon be dark. Our five children were playing happily outside, and the baby was playing nearby where we were working. Tabitha, age four, and Huldah, age two, were exploring near the barn, at the edge of the thick underbrush. Wild flowers grew in abundance, and Tabitha bent to pick a flower for me.

Suddenly, I heard the terrified screams of my two little girls. I dropped what I was doing and met them at the barn door. Trembling, they ran into my arms, clinging to me, and I wrapped my arms around them to comfort them.

What is wrong? All sorts of thoughts swirled through my brain. *What wild animal could have come out of the underbrush? Did a snake bite them, or a spider?*

At last, I understood their out-of-breath words. They said they heard a snake! Later, Tabitha informed me that when she bent to pick the flower, the noise started. Huldah later said, "Jesus told us to *run*!"

I smiled over their heads at my husband, who was observing from across the barn with a questioning look. I was sure my little girls' imaginations were getting away from them. They had no idea what a snake sounded like. Besides, I suspected I knew what it was. When they calmed down, I left them still sniffing at the barn entrance and went to check. Sure enough, I heard the sound as well.

"Don't worry," I called back. "It's just the cicadas. Come on over. Is this the sound you heard?" We listened to the buzzing noise of the insects.

"Yes," they agreed. Work and play resumed. Yet, I did wonder at the noise coming from the ground level and mentioned this to my husband.

"It would be interesting to check out what the cicadas are doing on the ground," I said. "Usually their noise comes from up in the trees." (All week, we had been hearing the roar of them around us, as it was time for them to come out from beneath the ground. It sounded like distant highway traffic, it was so loud. At any time, these insects with their big, red eyes would come out, shedding their shell casing and the males would noisily start calling for the females to begin mating).

Five minutes later, my husband went to check out the cicadas himself. He was looking around the tree and did not discover cicadas, but instead, a rattlesnake loudly warning of his location! He calmly called our oldest son to bring a shovel, and soon the loud rattling was quiet. Our little family stood around, staring in awe at the four-foot-long rattlesnake that hung off of my husband's shovel.

The little girls were right! It really had been a snake! Yet, what made them think so? Or *who*? They had not *seen* the snake but merely heard the noise of its rattling. They had never heard that noise before, and it really did sound similar to the cicadas they had been hearing all week.

We knelt that evening and thanked the Lord for His protection over our little girls. Could it be that God sent His angels to tell the girls it was a snake and they should run away? If my husband had not gone to check, we never would have known that the snake was there. Had he been prompted by the Lord to go check? The Lord is merciful, and we are thankful for His protection and care over us! *"For He shall give His angels charge over thee, to keep thee in all thy ways." Psalm 91:11.* ❧

Janet Overholt, 2015
Sarasota, FL

Try Out Your Math

➢ What was the number of angels John saw around the throne of God besides the thousands of thousands?

_____ Revelation 5:11

➢ How many angels could Jesus have called to rescue Him from the armed, religious leaders and multitude that came to arrest Him?

_____ Matthew 26:53

- Vera Overholt

45

Woke by an Angel

"And the angel...waked me..." Zechariah 4:1

I was driving one day to visit my son, Larry, at the hospital about two hours away. I often went alone to visit him, so the trip was not unusual – except that I was feeling so sleepy. I never had trouble staying awake while driving, and always asked God for His angels to watch over me and help me to drive safely. I would sing and talk to God as I drove.

But on that particular day, after driving only a short distance, I began to feel sleepy. Finally, I stopped and got out and walked around my car a couple of times.

I was soon wide awake again, so I got in the car and resumed driving. Then I saw the sign, "Two miles to Clinton," and was relieved that I was about at the hospital.

I don't remember becoming sleepy again. But suddenly, it felt as though something was punching me on both sides! I jumped and looked ahead, and was terrified to see my car headed into the oncoming lane! I yanked my steering wheel to the right just in time to miss the oncoming car as it passed. I was certain it was God's angel that woke me up at that moment and I began thanking Him for His protection.

But, where was I? By then I should have arrived in Clinton, a good-sized town. As I drove on, I soon discovered that I was a couple of miles farther than Clinton! *Oh, I drove through the town and didn't remember driving through it! How long was I sleeping?*

Had you been along that day, you would have heard a praise service the remainder of the way to the hospital! Again, God was on time and the angels did their job well. Praise His holy name. ❧

Mary Keely, 2016
Sturgis, MI

But we see Jesus,
who was made
a little lower than the angels
for the suffering of death,
crowned with glory and honor;
that He by the grace of God
should taste death for every man.
For verily He took not on Him
the nature of angels;
but He took on Him
the seed of Abraham.
Hebrews 2:9

Angels of the Bible – Quiz

The Bible often speaks of angels and the messages they brought. Following is a list of visits and messages. On the blanks, write the names of the people involved.

1. I was sleeping under a juniper tree when an angel touched me and said, "Arise and eat." _____ (I Kings 19:1-8)

2. I was cast among hungry lions. God sent an angel to shut their mouths so that I could spend all night without being harmed. _____ (Daniel 6:22)

3. I fled from my angry mistress. An angel found me in the wilderness and told me to return to my mistress. He also told me I would have a son soon. _____ (Genesis 16:7-11)

4. I was a prisoner on a boat. An angel stood by me one night and told me that no one on the boat would lose his life in the shipwreck. _____ (Acts 27)

5. My wife was in the field when the angel came to her. She hastened to come for me. Our special message was that we would have a son who would be a Nazarite and would deliver Israel from the Philistines. _____ (Judges 13:1-14)

6. Two angels came to me one evening when I was sitting at the gate of the city. They told me to take my family and leave the city, for it would be destroyed. _____ (Genesis 19:1-14)

7. The Lord and two angels came to visit us one warm day. We quickly prepared a meal for them. The Lord told us that within the year we would have a son, even though we were very old. _____ (Genesis 18:1-14)

CONTINUED ON NEXT PAGE

8. I was threshing wheat with my father when an angel found me. He told me to save Israel from the Midianites. _____ (Judges 6:11-24)

9. I was young and unmarried when the angel Gabriel brought me a very special message: I was to be the mother of the promised Messiah! _____ (Luke 1:26-35)

10. I was the centurion of the Italian band – a Gentile. I saw an angel in a vision, who told me to send to Joppa for a man named Simon Peter. He would tell me what to do. _____ (Acts 10:1-33)

11. On the first day of the week we went to see the grave where the body of our Master had been laid. An angel had rolled back the stone and was sitting on it. He told us that Jesus had risen, and we were to go and tell His disciples. _____ (Matthew 28:1-8)

12. An angel came and revealed wonderful things to me while I was on the Isle of Patmos. _____ (Revelation 1)

13. In a dream I saw a ladder that had angels ascending and descending on it. The Lord promised me that night that the land where I slept would belong to my descendants. _____ (Genesis 28:10-13)

14. An angel came to me in a dream one night and told me not to be afraid to take Mary, my betrothed, to me. _____ (Matthew 1:18-25)

15. I was riding my donkey when suddenly it refused to go on. Then my eyes were opened, and I saw an angel in my path. _____ (Numbers 22:22-35)

CONTINUED ON NEXT PAGE

16. I went into the inner part of the temple to offer incense. An angel came and told me that my wife would have a son in her old age. When I refused to believe it, I could not speak until after this promised was fulfilled._____ (Lu. 1:5-64)

17. I was watching my father-in-law's flock when an angel spoke to me out of a burning bush and told me to go to the king and ask him to let my people leave the country. _____ (Exodus 3:1-10)

18. We were keeping watch over our flocks when the angel of the Lord came to us and told us about a wonderful birth. _____ (Luke 2:7-12)

19. We were with Jesus on Mount Olivet. Jesus ascended into heaven, and the angel told us that someday He would return in like manner as we had seem Him go. _____ (Acts 1:1-12)

20. An angel told me to go to a desert on the road to Gaza, and preach to an Ethiopian riding on a chariot. _____ (Acts 8:26-39)

21. When I was in prison, an angel came and awoke me and led me to freedom. _____ (Acts 12:1-17)

Garnete Steiner
Apple Creek, Ohio
Used by permission.

ANGEL QUIZ ANSWERS

1. Elijah 2. Daniel 3. Hagar 4. Paul 5. Manoah 6. Lot 7. Abraham 8. Sarah & Gideon 9. Mary 10. Cornelius 11. Mary and Mary Magdalene 12. John 13. Jacob 14. Joseph 15. Balaam 16. Zacharias 17. Moses 18. Shepherds 19. The Apostles 20. Philip 21. Peter

God Himself is present, hear the praise resounding!
See the host the throne surrounding!
"Holy, Holy, Holy," hear the hymn ascending,
Angels, saints, their voices blending!

O thou Fount of blessing, purify my spirit,
Trusting only in Thy merit;
Like the holy angels who behold Thy glory,
May I ceaselessly adore Thee.

God Himself is Present - Gerhard Tersteegen, 1729
#10 The Christian Hymnary

ANGELS FROM THE REALMS OF GLORY

James Montgomery, 1816

Henry Smart, 1867

1. An gels, from the realms of glo - ry, Wing your flight o'er all the earth,
2. Shepherds, in the field a - bid - ing, Watch-ing o'er your flocks by night,
3. Sa - ges, leave your con - tem - pla - tions, Bright - er vi - sions beam a - far;
4. Saints, be - fore the al - tar bend-ing, Watch-ing long in hope and fear,
5. Sin - ners, wrung with true re - pent-ance, Doom'd for guilt to end - less pains,

Ye who sang cre - a - tion's sto - ry, Now pro-claim Mes - si - ah's birth;
God with man is now re - sid - ing, Yon - der shines the in - fant light;
Seek the great de - sire of na - tions; Ye have seen His na - tal star;
Sud - den - ly the Lord de - scend-ing In His tem - ple shall ap - pear;
Jus - tice now re - vokes the sen - tence, Mer - cy calls you, break your chains;

Come and wor - ship, Come and wor - ship Wor - ship Christ the new-born King.

CHARIOTS OF FIRE SURROUNDING ME

The Lord opened the eyes of the young man, and he saw: and behold, the
mountain was full of horses and chariots of fire round about Elisha. II Kings 6:17

Michael Overholt, 1989 (b. 1972)   Michael Overholt

Chorus

Char - iots of fire sur-round-ing me, An - gels a - wait - ing God's com -

mand; I have no need to fear for my Lord is near, Char - iots of

fine

fire sur-round-ing me.
1. When the temp - ter comes with all his might,
2. Sa - tan can - not win a - gainst his foe,
3. There's pro - tec - tion in the arms of God,

Draw - ing me from my Lord and King; I need strength to go
I have arm - ies pro - tect - ing me; Like E - li - sha in -
There is heal - ing there for your soul; He will keep His sheep

D. C.

and to guide me right, Char - iots of fire sur - round - ing me.
side the cit - y walls,
safe thru all the storms,

192

HE SHALL GIVE HIS ANGELS CHARGE OVER THEE

Psalm 91: 11, 12
Refrain from Genesis 24:40

Vera Overholt, 2015 (b. 1931)
Har. by Overholt family

He shall give His an-gels charge o-ver thee, To keep thee in all thy ways. They shall bear thee up in their hands lest thou dash thy foot a-gainst a stone.

Refrain

Glo-ry hal-le-lu-jah! An-gels are with me, To pros-per and di-rect my way.

OPEN MY EYES THAT I MAY SEE

Open Thou mine eyes, that I may behold wondrous things out of Thy law. Psalm 119:18.

Vera Sommers Overholt (b. 1931)

Vera Sommers Overholt

1. O - pen my eyes that I may see An - gel - ic hosts sur-
II Kings 6:13-18
2. O - pen my eyes that I may see Riv - ers of wa - ter
Genesis 21:14-21
3. O - pen my eyes that I may see Thy won - drous laws — re-
Psalm 119:18

round - ing me; More are with me than Sa - tan's foes,
flow - ing free; My thirst to quench, my soul re - vive,
veal to me; I'll tell the world of Thy great Name,

CHORUS

No pow'r can e'er God's way op - pose. —
My faint - ing heart to sat - is - fy. — An - gel - ic hosts — sur-
Thy pre - cious Word I will pro - claim. —

round - ing — me, Help me, dear Lord, to trust in Thee; I would

clasp my hand — in Thine, Ev - — er safe, Thou Great Di - vine!

THE ANGEL OF THE LORD ENCAMPETH ROUND ABOUT

Psalm 34:7-8   Unknown

The an - gel of the Lord en - camp - eth round a - bout them that

fear Him, and de - liv - 'reth them. them. O taste and see

that the Lord is good: Bless - ed is the man that

trust - eth in Him. O taste and see that the Lord

is good: Bless - ed is the man that trust - eth in Him.

WHILE SHEPHERDS WATCHED THEIR FLOCKS

Lk. 2:8-14
Nahum Tate, 1703

George F. Handel, 1728

1. While shep-herds watched their flocks by night, All seat-ed
2. "Fear not!" said he; for might-y dread Had seized their
3. "To you, in Da-vid's town, this day Is born, of
4. "The heav'n-ly babe you there shall find To hu-man
5. Thus spake the se-raph; and forth-with Ap-peared a
6. "All glo-ry be to God on high, And to the

on the ground, The an-gel of the Lord came down,
troub-led mind; "Glad ti-dings of great joy I bring,
Da-vid's line, The Sav-iour, who is Christ the Lord,
view dis-played, All mean-ly wrapped in swath-ing-bands,
shin-ing throng Of an-gels prais-ing God on high,
earth be peace: Good will hence-forth from heav'n to men,

And glo-ry shone a-round, And glo-ry shone a-round.
To you and all man-kind, To you and all man-kind.
And this shall be the sign:— And this shall be the sign:—
And in a man-ger laid, And in a man-ger laid."
Who thus ad-dressed their song:— Who thus ad-dressed their song:—
Be-gin and nev-er cease! Be-gin and nev-er cease!"

"*A*re they not all
ministering spirits,
Sent Forth to Minister
for them who shall be
heirs of salvation?"

Hebrews 1:14

To God be the glory!

Fellowservants!

*"And I, John, saw these things, and heard them.
And when I had heard and seen,
I fell down to worship before the feet of the angel
which shewed me these things.*

*Then saith he unto me, 'See thou do it not:
for I am thy fellowservant,
and of thy brethren the prophets,
and of them which keep the sayings of this book:
worship God.'"* Revelation 22:8, 9

Quizzes